MW00632576

To the Eskim
who gave us the kayak, a gift of continuing relevance
and pleasure

QAYAQ

Kayaks of Alaska and Siberia

David W. Zimmerly

Paul Gardinier, Kayak Exhibit Coordinator

University of Alaska Press
Fairbanks, Alaska

Library of Congress Cataloging-in-Publication Data

Zimmerly, David W., 1938–
    QAYAQ: kayaks of Alaska and Siberia / David W. Zimmerly ; Paul Gardinier, kayak
exhibit coordinator.
        p. cm.
    Includes bibliographical references and index.
    ISBN 1–889963–10–0 (alk. paper)
    1. Eskimos--Alaska--Boats--Exhibitions. 2. Ethnology--Russia (Federations)--Siberia,
Northeastern--Exhibitions. 3. Kayaks--Alaska--Exhibitions. 4. Kayaks--Russia
(Federation)--Siberia, Northeastern--Exhibitions.

E99.E7 Z56 2000
387.2'o--dc21   00-027096

Second Edition, 2000, published by:
University of Alaska Press
P.O. Box 756240
Fairbanks, AK 99775-6240
(907) 474-5831
fypress@uaf.edu
www.uaf.edu/uapress

First Edition, 1986, published by:
Alaska State Museum
Division of State Museums
Department of Education
395 Whittier Street
Juneau, AK 99801

International Standard Book Number:
        1–889963–10–0
Library of Congress Catalog Number: 00-027096

Printed in the United States by Data Reproductions
Corporation.

Publication coordination by Pamela Odom and
production by Deirdre Helfferich, University of
Alaska Press.

Cover design by Dixon Jones, Rasmuson Library
Graphics, University of Alaska Fairbanks.
Book design by Elizabeth Knecht.

Front Cover:

Vu d'isle de St. Paul de la mer de Kamtchatka (View of Island of St. Paul from the Sea of Kamchatka), lithograph by Louis Choris, from his book *Vues et paysages des régions équinoxiales,* **first published in 1826.**

Louis Choris was the offical painter of the 1815–18 Russian around-the-world voyage, under the command of Otto von Kotzebue. He made many drawings during the expedition which he was encouraged to publish upon his return to Paris. *Vues et paysages des régions équinoxiales* **became a valuable work on Alaska, California and the Sandwich (Hawaiian) Islands.**

Collection Alaska Historical Library.

Publisher's Note

This book accompanied an exhibit held at the Alaska State Museum in the summer of 1986 and at the Anchorage Museum of History and Art in the spring of 1987. The UA Press has altered author Zimmerly's spelling of the word kayak, *"qajaq,"* in the original edition for the Yupik spelling *"qayaq,"* most commonly seen in Alaska.

CONTENTS

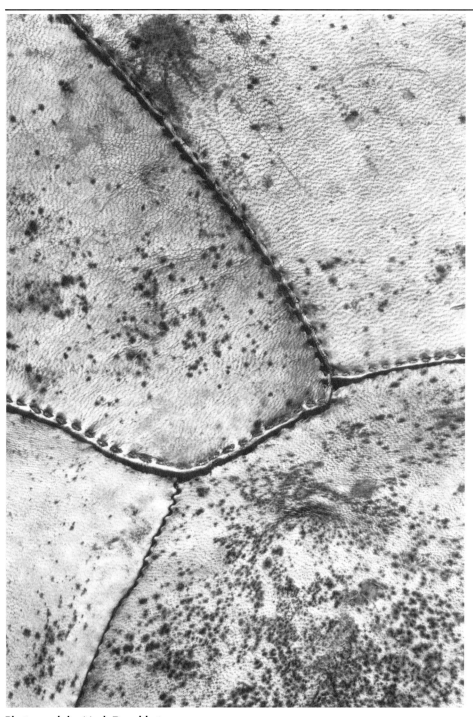

Photograph by Mark Daughhetee

PREFACE TO THE 2000 EDITION   vi
PREFACE TO THE 1986 EDITION   viii
ACKNOWLEDGEMENTS   ix
INTRODUCTION   3
KAYAK DESIGN   5
SIBERIA   9
  Koryak
  Chukchi
  Siberian Eskimo
ALEUT   15
PACIFIC ESKIMO   29
  Kodiak Eskimo
  Chugach Eskimo
BERING SEA   39
  Nunivak/Hooper Bay
  Norton Sound
BERING STRAIT   53
  Cape Espenberg
  King Island
NORTH ALASKA   63
  Kotzebue Sound/Point Barrow
  North Alaska Retrieval Kayak
  Nunamiut
MACKENZIE ESKIMO   71
PADDLES   77
CONCLUSIONS   83
GLOSSARY   85
REFERENCES CITED   91
INDEX   96

PREFACE TO THE 2000 EDITION

In the summer of 1986, shortly after the exhibition, *Qajaq: Kayaks of Siberia and Alaska,* opened at the Alaska State Museum in Juneau, my wife Helga and I set off in *Erasmus,* our cruising sailboat to see the world from the water.

One of the fascinating aspects of our journey was to see the variety of small working craft used by different cultures. On the Labrador coast we admired the sturdy dories used to set and haul cod traps. On Baffin Island, where we first wintered, the vessels of choice were square-stern freighter canoes with powerful outboards. The Inuit used them for hunting seal or transporting families to summer fishing camps. It was not until we reached Africa that we found small working craft powered by man. Anchored in a deep, protected inlet in Kenya, we were awakened by the melodic working chant of two fishermen paddling a roughly hewn dugout canoe past *Erasmus.*

Seeing first-hand the varied solutions for water transport developed in other areas reinforced my respect for the craftsmanship and design of Eskimo kayaks. The design modifications made for local conditions and needs resulted in a variety of kayak types each superbly suited for subsistence living.

Returning to North America after ten years, I found that a passion for sea kayaking and a fascination with traditional kayak types had grown during the decade. Enthusiasts continue to refine their knowledge of Native design and construction by building and testing replicas of aboriginal kayak types. This trend makes my years of research and documentation worth far more than academic interest.

To my knowledge, there remains much work to be done in this area. Many interesting museum specimens, such as the Koryak, the inland and seagoing Chukchi, and the Mackenzie kayak types have yet to be replicated.

The Mackenzie Eskimo kayak was not included in the original edition of *Qajaq.* However, it is so closely related to the Alaska types that it seems fitting to include it with its near-relatives rather than with other Canadian Inuit types.

In Canada the word Inuit has replaced Eskimo in common usage. This is correct in Canada, and, for the most part, in Greenland. However, both Inuit and Yuit people live in Alaska and Siberia. The word Eskimo encompasses all Inuit and Yuit cultural groups.

An Alaska Eskimo hunting for seal in the Bering Straits. From *Across Arctic America* (Rasmussen 1927, 345).

Groupings, while correct from an anthropological aspect do not necessarily conform to local usage. Spelling, too, is problematic, with local variants. Yuit, Yupik, or Yupíik, for example are all correct. In the title of this publication, *qajaq* has been changed from a Canadian spelling to the more common Alaska spelling, *qayaq*.

My years on the water left me with a respect for the sea in all its awesome aspects. I took my own east arctic kayak replica with me on the deck of my sailboat and experienced some of the grandeur of paddling off the Labrador and Baffin Island coasts. The bones of that kayak remain in Cape Dorset. More recently Helga and I discovered the pleasures of paddling our two-person folding kayak in the Atlantic swell off the coast of Maine. Hypalon, cordura, and aircraft aluminum have replaced painted canvas and wood, yet I could again feel the kayak working with the sea. The modern and the traditional can make a fine marriage.

A kayak should be a dynamic entity, not just a museum specimen. I am grateful to all of you who keep traditional kayaks alive.

David W. Zimmerly

PREFACE TO THE 1986 EDITION

The arctic kayak appeals to us on an emotional level beyond that inspired by more prosaic items of material culture. It has a romantic image associated with fur-clad Eskimos silently gliding along, hunting their sustenance or playing like otters in the waves; it illustrates the artistry and ingenuity of man in fashioning a superior means of transportaion in an unforgiving climate. But perhaps we relate to the kayak on an even deeper level—it represents a means of man becoming at one with the rhythms of the sea; and as a means of transportation, it represents a singular image of freedom.

Qajaq: Kayaks of Siberia and Alaska is a major exhibit by the Alaska State Museum that examines the arctic kayak and its use and importance to historic arctic cultures. This book was conceived as support and enhancement for the exhibit which appears in Juneau and Anchorage during 1986 and 1987.

Qajaq is the first comprehensive exhibit of Alaskan kayaks ever organized. The exhibit is organized on a geographical basis to show the design differences of Siberian and Alaskan kayaks. All major styles of Alaskan and Siberian kayaks are represented with models, line drawings, historical photographs, or actual full-sized kayaks and associated equipment.

This book includes many line drawings, historical photographs, and drawings from the exhibit. In addition there is more text and bibliographic material in the book than was possible to present in the exhibit.

As an anthropologist I have been documenting kayaks and the cultures that used them for the last 15 years. My research of kayaks has taken me to museums and archives from California to Leningrad. I have lived and paddled with Eskimos from Baffin Island to Alaska and I have spent countless days and nights making and paddling reconstructions of arctic kayaks.

I have both an academic and personal involvement with the study of kayaks. My interest combines an intense intellectual fascination for the history and technology of the craft with a strong emotional attachment. But perhaps it is the latter attraction that best allows us to relate to peoples of the past.

David W. Zimmerly

ACKNOWLEDGEMENTS

The Qajaq project—exhibition and book—has been a major undertaking for this museum which has called upon the talents and resources of a number of individuals and institutions. Primary among these is David Zimmerly, who authored this book and whose many years of research form the structure for the exhibition. David provided the consultation and direction we needed to give substance to our ideas. His kayak research was generously supported by the National Museums of Canada from 1971 to 1982 when he was the arctic ethnologist at the National Museum of Man in Ottawa. Kenneth DeRoux, curator of Visual Arts at the Alaska State Museum, has collaborated with me on this project from the very beginning, providing backup support and tying up loose ends. The kayaks in the collection of the Sheldon Jackson Museum form the core of this exhibit. Other lenders to the exhibit to whom thanks are due include: the University of Alaska Museum in Fairbanks, the Lowie Museum of Anthropology at the University of California in Berkeley, the Thomas Burke Memorial Washington State Museum in Seattle, and R.T. Wallen of Juneau, whose collection and enthusiasm sparked my initial interest in traditional kayaks.

Transportation of the kayaks themselves has been a major part of the exhibit logistics, and for this special thanks are due the United States Coast Guard and Lts. Woodcock and Bratner, who transported two of the kayaks from Anchorage to Juneau. Mitchell Gaul and Gene Motes of the Anchorage Museum of History and Art were also instrumental in making these arrangements, with the support of their museum's director, Robert Shalkop.

Another key player assisting with the careful transportation of the loan items has been Don Tucker of Alaska Marine Lines, who graciously donated van transportation from Seattle.

Important financial support for the exhibition book has been provided by the Friends of the Alaska State Museum, whose dedicated support of museum activities continues to play an important role in almost all that we do.

A number of individuals deserve special thanks for their contributions. Joe Lubischer of Seattle provided valuable information with regard to the "speed secrets" in Aleut kayaks and assisted with the selection of these items from the Thomas Burke Memorial Washington State Museum. Chris Cunningham constructed two beautiful models of Siberian kayaks for the show, as full-size examples of these were not available. Chris also graciously loaned his full-size King Island kayak replica for use by John Heath in describing traditional Eskimo and Inuit techniques of paddling and rolling kayaks. John has provided enthusiastic support and information for the project. Scott Brylinsky and Ron Ripple demonstrated a number of traditional Alaska and Greenlandic kayak survival methods, providing us the opportunity to see some ways that kayaks were safely used. Laura Lucas and Bob Banghart ably assisted museum staff with the late night marathon exhibit installation.

Phyllis DeMuth and Verda Carey at the Alaska Historical Library provided assistance in locating many of the historical photos and illustrations for the catalog and exhibit. Diane Brenner at the Anchorage Museum of History and Art also located historical photos.

The Public Information staff at the Department of Education, State of Alaska, also deserve credit for their role in bringing this project to fruition. In particular, I mention Mark Daughhetee and Kyoko Ikenoue. Mark did most of the artifact photography for the catalog as well as the hand-colored illustration and design for the poster, and Kyoko saved us a lot of production time by doing the typesetting. Chris Yarrow, Marge Hermans, and data processing whiz Alice Baroo have all contributed in the area of compiling the catalog text.

Finally, I thank the staff of the Alaska State Museum and the Sheldon Jackson Museum, almost all of whom have contributed to this project in one way or another. Central among them have been: Elizabeth Knecht, graphic designer, who has supervised the production of this book and related graphic materials and has been directly involved in the installation of the show; Cheryl McLean, who has worked on proofreading and editing; Bruce Kato, curator of exhibits, who has provided input and assistance all along and has been directly involved in the installation of the show; Alice Hoveman, conservator for her help with the installation and mounting of artifacts; and Marcia Wilcox, who helped in cleaning the kayaks prior to exhibit. Volunteer Louise Martin has ably handled much of the publicity for the exhibit.

Thanks are also due to Lynn Wallen, curator of collections, and Judy Hauck, registrar; and to the interpretation and outreach staff, Betty Bradlyn, curator, for arranging special events and publicity, and Jerry Howard, who gave us a hand with the installation.

Of course none of this could be accomplished without administrative support. Olive Ratcliffe has helped immeasurably and always cheerfully, processing the steady stream of paperwork we have generated. She has been ably assisted by Jolie Sasseville and Deborah Leamer, who have helped not only with the accounting work and travel arrangements, but also with word processing.

Bette Hulbert, director of the Sheldon Jackson Museum, and Perter Corey, curator, have supported the idea of this exhibit from its inception and have graciously put up with seeing the museum's kayaks go out on loan for a longer period of time than they had expected. For this we are very grateful. Initial and continued support has also come from Alan Munro, deputy director at the Alaska State Museum, and last but certainly not least, from our new director, Thomas Lonner, who came on in midstream and whose enthusiastic support has expanded the scope of the project and cleared the way around many obstacles.

Paul Gardinier
Kayak Exhibit Coordinator

QAYAQ

Kayaks of Alaska and Siberia

INTRODUCTION

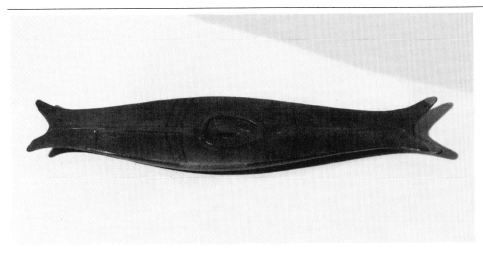

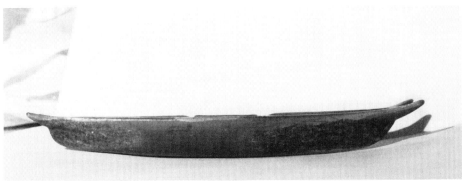

Figures 1 & 2. 2,000 year-old Siberian kayak model exhibiting features common to an umiak and to Chukchi inland kayaks.

There are few watercraft with a history as old as that of kayaks. Archaeological evidence for kayaks shows them to be at least 2,000 years old. Further inferential evidence places their origins back another 2,000 years and I would not be surprised to find the total age of the kayak to be over 5,000 years.

One of the problems in trying to date kayaks is that, because they are skin-covered, sinew-lashed and wood-framed, they do not survive the vagaries of time well. It is no surprise that no complete archaeological specimens have been found intact. Archaeologists instead look for items that are usually associated with kayaks such as bird darts, throwing boards, double-bladed paddles, ivory kayak fittings and so forth. Evidence of this sort is found in the Aleutian Islands where pre-Aleut sites date back to 1700 B.C.

At a Seward Peninsula site with excellent preservation, Danish archaeologist Helge Larsen unearthed a piece of sealskin kayak cover. Dating back to around 0 A.D. it was preserved enough to see the markings of the kayak's longitudinal stringers establishing that the kayak was multi-chined, the same as those of recent times.

Preserved kayak models dating back two millennia were found in a cemetery near East Cape, Siberia. One of the models exhibits characteristics that link it to the umiak, the open skin boat found across the Arctic. The design of the contemporary Chukchi inland kayak also preserves umiak construction features. It is very probable that the kayak is a descendant of the umiak.

Russian linguist G. A. Menovshchikov thinks differently. He studied the etymology of Eskimo-Aleut boat terms. He believes that the proto-Eskimo/proto-Aleut linguistic split took place 4,000 to 5,000 years ago and that the kayak and umiak existed side by side from the beginning (1976:112, 116).

The kayak model shown in Figures 1 and 2 exhibits these umiak-like features of form and end shapes. The model almost appears to be a small decked-over umiak.

I distinguish the kayak from a canoe or other small craft through the following definition: **KAYAK**—a small watercraft composed of a discrete wooden framework covered and decked-over with skin and generally supplied with individual cockpits for one to three occupants. The paddlers are usually in a sitting position with outstretched legs and most frequently use double-bladed paddles.

Before European contact, kayaks were used by all Eskimo groups, the Aleutian Islanders and the Koryak and Chukchi peoples of Siberia. The craft was mainly used to hunt seals, walrus and whales. But it also served to hunt caribou in inland lakes and rivers, to fish and tend fishing nets, to ferry people across streams, to catch birds and to pursue many other activities.

Today kayaks are in use only in extreme north and south Greenland and a few communities in southwest Alaska, replaced elsewhere by commercial outboard-equipped square-stern canoes and other motorboats.

Kayaks have not survived as a viable hunting craft through the end of the 20th century, and it is doubtful that they will survive even as museum specimens. There are only 200 to 300 kayaks still surviving in museums around the world. Because of their size, materials and weight, they are the most delicate artifact in many museum collections and consequently are deteriorating rapidly. Incorrectly stored on their fragile hull bottoms, the kayak's weight eventually forces the bottom up, breaking the ribs. Large changes in temperature and humidity cause the skin cover to shrink and either rip the cover or crush the wooden skeleton.

But before kayaks are completely gone we do have a chance to gain an understanding of them from exhibits and publications. In this book we will take a look at the construction of various Alaskan and Siberian kayaks and show how the shapes and uses varied depending on climate and available resources. We will also look at associated equipment such as paddles, harpoons and clothing, study the hunting techniques developed over the years and delve into some of the specialized construction techniques of certain builders.

David W. Zimmerly
Ottawa
June 1986

KAYAK DESIGN

The climatic and topographic conditions under which kayaks evolved varied widely. In southern Greenland or Alaska, the waters remained ice-free virtually year-round. The High Arctic offered only a 90-day respite from the ever-present ice. As the conditions varied, so did the kayaks. Currently, evidence of some 40 different native kayak designs has been catalogued.

There were two main uses for kayaks: kayaks used in sheltered inland lakes and rivers for pursuing caribou and those used in the open ocean to hunt sea mammals.

Inland Kayaks

The inland kayaks had to be swift enough to catch up with fast-swimming caribou (up to 5 knots). The epitome of this type is found inland of the west coast of Hudson Bay among the Caribou Eskimo.

Their kayaks were long (up to 30 feet), with narrow beam (as little as 15 inches), and multi-chined (round-bottomed) with enough rocker to enable fast escape from an angry wounded caribou.

The round bottom is important as it gives the least wetted surface area which lowers frictional resistance with the water.

The Caribou Eskimo kayak had a long sharply aft-raked stern which caused the kayak to weathercock bow to wind, perhaps useful in requiring the least effort to stay downwind of a small group of caribou.

Speed and maneuverability, then, were the basic design factors for this important kayak use and the same basic criteria were met by kayaks used in North Alaska, the Mackenzie River area and Keewatin areas of Canada.

Sea Kayaks

The requirements for a sea mammal hunting kayak were quite different. Because a frightened seal will dive and be gone in an instant, stealth, not speed, was the important design characteristic for this class of kayaks. Paddles were purposely made long and narrow to decrease dripping water noises while maintaining a high wetted surface for power paddling.

Figure 3. "Eskimaux Killing Deer in a Lake," from W.E. Parry's *Journal of a second voyage for the discovery of a Northwest passage*, 1824. Steel engraving from a drawing by G. F. Lyon.

The boats also had to be seaworthy; the windswept Arctic coasts demanded no less. Finally, such boats had to be able to carry home captured game, sometimes over considerable distances. These seagoing kayaks came in four basic forms, though slight changes in response to local conditions were common.

- The Greenland Eskimos designed low-profile, low-volume sea kayaks with a needle shape and upswept ends. Typically 17 to 18 feet long, these narrow (about 19-inch) hard-chined boats with their V-bottom cross sections demanded the utmost skill from a paddler. These boats required that their paddler continually balance with either paddle or body movements. The Greenlanders responded with over 25 capsize recovery techniques, both self- and team-rescue tactics. With his watertight sealskin parka sealed tightly around the cockpit rim, wrists, and head, the kayaker faced capsizing with relatively little trepidation.

The boats' ultra-low profile shed the Arctic gales well and was difficult to spot from a seal's-eye view. But the low, flat decks offered little carrying capacity for captured game. Instead, the Greenland hunters usually towed their quarry home using complex toggle systems.

- The Baffin Islanders, who also hunted sea mammals, solved the seaworthiness/carrying capacity problem in a second, far different manner. They built wide, flat-bottomed kayaks that were so stable that capsize recovery techniques were not needed or at least not learned. These most stable of all Arctic kayaks had flared sides and high cockpit coamings, nearly eliminating the need for a spray skirt. They had great game-carrying capacity atop their broad, flat afterdecks — up to 1,000 pounds. The design is rather agile, but requires hard paddling.

- From the Bering Strait south to the Aleutians, native kayaks exhibited a third solution to the general problem. Short (15-16 feet), with generous beam (up to 29 inches), these boats had flattened bottoms, multiple chines and moderate flare to the topsides. This fairly stable cross section was combined with raised (peaked) decks to efficiently shed water in a rough sea.

But carrying game on deck raised the center of gravity too high for good stability. The solution: the Bering Sea and Strait hunters butchered their game on a nearby icefloe, then stuffed it into the kayak ends with special gaffs and hooked implements. These boats' other unusual feature came in the form of a single-bladed paddle. A limited number of single-blade capsize recovery techniques were known and used.

Figure 4. "View of Island of St. Paul from the Sea of Kamchatka." Colored lithograph by Louis Choris from his *Voyage pittoresque autour du monde*, 1822. Collection Alaska Historical Library.

Alaska and Siberian Kayak Average Measurements

Kayak Type	Length (ft.)/ Sample size	Beam (in.)	Depth (in.)	Weight (lbs.)
Koryak	9.2' / 4	27.8"	10.1"	43.4
Chukchi	15.2' / 4	22.1"	10.8"	35.5
Asiatic Eskimo	No Known Specimens			
Aleut				
One-hole	17.4' / 14	19.3"	12.0"	36.4
Two-hole	20.7' / 5	23.2"	12.4"	47.4
Three-hole	24.7' / 4	28.2"	13.6"	–
Kodiak Eskimo				
One-hole	14.3' / 3	27.1"	11.2"	–
Two-hole	19.6' / 2	29.3"	12.8"	–
Three-hole	24.7' / 3	30.3"	15.3"	–
Chugach Eskimo				
Three-hole	20.9' / 2	28.0"	–	–
Bering Sea				
Bristol Bay	15.6' / 3	27.7"	15.0"	66.1
Nunivak Island				
Hooper Bay	15.4' / 9	29.3"	13.5"	58.4
Norton Sound	16.5' / 7	25.9"	13.8"	58.8
Bering Strait				
King Island				
Cape Prince of Wales	14.9' / 9	24.6"	13.2"	38.6
Cape Espenberg				
Two-hole	18.0' / –	27.5"	19.0"	96.1
North Alaska				
Cape Krusenstern				
Point Hope				
Point Barrow	17.7' / 3	19.7"	8.6"	27.4
Nunamiut				
Retrieval	9.6' / 1	23.2"	7.6"	24.9
Mackenzie	15.75" / 8	19.2"	8.1"	33.5

- The Aleut and Koryak peoples developed a fourth solution. Though their respective kayaks were very dissimilar looking, both types used rock ballast carried low in the hull to improve stability. Evidently, the ballast worked; neither group relied on capsize self-recovery techniques.

The Koryaks of Siberia used very short (9 to 10 feet), beamy (28-inch) V-bottom craft and simply did not use them in difficult water and weather conditions.

The Aleuts ranged the cold, rainy Aleutian Islands in far more capable boats. They were renowned for paddling 10 miles or more out to sea, often for over 12 hours. They usually traveled in pairs and could "catamaran" together for stability in heavy weather. They carried water in bladder containers that could also double, after being inflated with air, as float bags. The float bags were either stuffed into the kayak ends or lashed on the gunwales outside near the cockpit.

The sleek and fast Aleut kayaks were a match for all others in the Arctic. Hulls were around 17–19 feet long, multichined with a moderate V-bottom. They also featured raised, wave-shedding decks.

In this book we will examine the inland-type kayak found among the Siberian Chukchi and North Alaskan Eskimos, the broad, beamy and stable Bering Sea and Bering Strait kayaks and the ballasted, more unstable types of the Koryak and Aleut.

Figure 5.

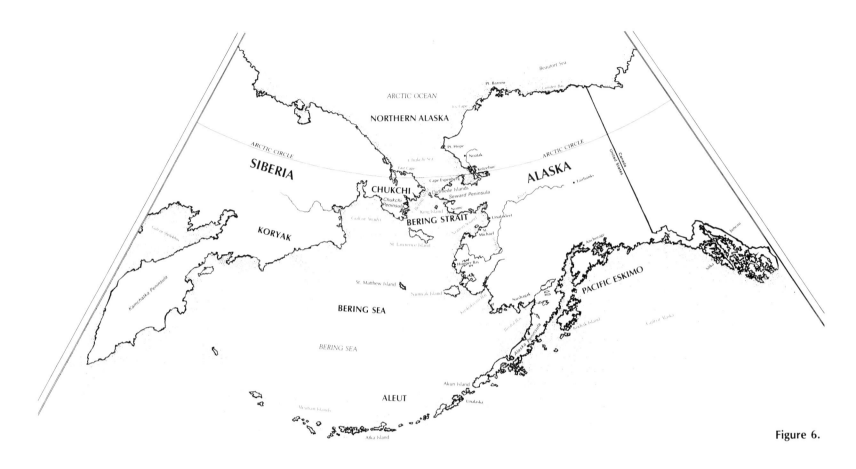

ARCTIC OCEAN

Beaufort Sea

Pt. Barrow

Camden Bay

NORTHERN ALASKA

Icy Cape

ARCTIC CIRCLE

Pt. Hope

Chukchi Sea

ARCTIC CIRCLE

SIBERIA

Noatak

Kotzebue

ALASKA

East Cape

Cape Espenberg

Diomede Islands

CHUKCHI

Fairbanks

Seward Peninsula

Chukchi
Peninsula

King Island

Nome

Canada
United States

Gulf of Anadyr

BERING STRAIT

Unalakleet

KORYAK

St.
Michael

Gulf of Shelekhov

St. Lawrence Island

Norton Sound

Hooper Bay

St. Matthew Island

Anchorage

PACIFIC ESKIMO

Kamchatka Peninsula

Nunivak Island

Sitka

Juneau

BERING SEA

Nushagak

Bristol Bay

Kodiak Island

Gulf of Alaska

BERING SEA

Alaska Peninsula

Akun Island

Unalaska

ALEUT

Aleutian Islands

Atka Island

Figure 6.

8

Figure 7. Lines and construction drawings of a Koryak kayak. Length 10′ 6″. Museum of Ethnography, Leningrad. Sheet (1 of 1). Line drawing IV-G-4M © Canadian Museum of Civilization.

The least known of all Arctic kayaks are those from Siberia made by the Koryak, Chukchi and Siberian Eskimo. By the time of the Russian Revolution, these kayaks were all but extinct with only a few specimens saved in museum collections. To my knowledge there are only four or five Chukchi and three Koryak kayaks in museum collections, and no Siberian Eskimo types.

Much of the primary source material on these people is written in Russian and stored in various archives in Leningrad. Other information is in travelers' and explorers' journals found only in rare book collections. The standard work in English on the Koryak is that of Jochelson (1908), and on the Chukchi by Bogoras (1909). Only scattered bits and pieces are to be found on the Siberian Eskimo.

Koryak

The Koryak people, sometimes called the Kamshadal, lived on both shores of the Kamchatka Peninsula. Their kayak was at once the smallest

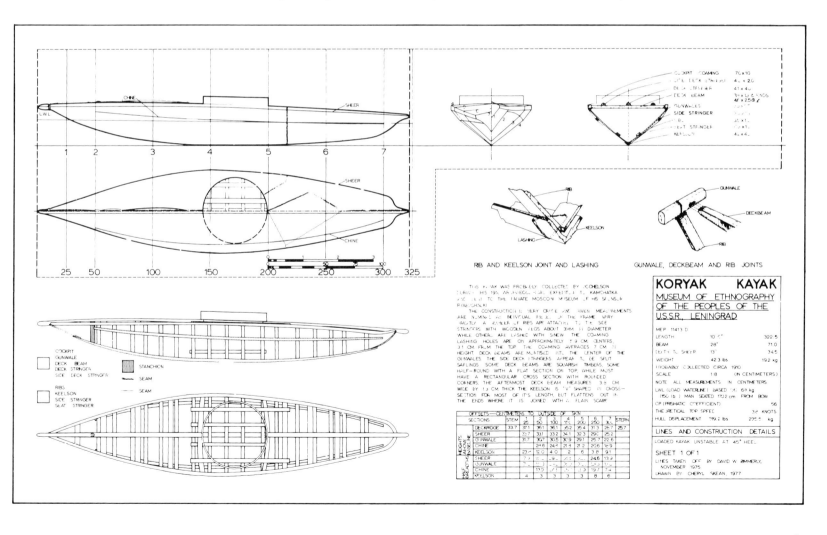

and the crudest-built of all kayaks, but still well-designed as a hunting craft for use in protected waters. Adney and Chapelle found the form "...much like the hunting and fowling skiffs former-ly used in America" (1964:195).

The Koryak kayak is short, beamy and V-bottomed as shown in Figure 7. This specimen, now in a Leningrad museum, was probably collected by Jochelson in Kamchatka around 1910. An 8' 5.8" Koryak kayak, also collected by Jochelson and stored in another museum in Leningrad, is shown in Figures 8 and 9.

The framework follows basic kayak construction with the two gunwales being the main strength members. They are held apart with deck beams let into the gunwale sides. Ribs are also let into the gunwales and then attached to the keelson. Longitudinal side stringers and deck stringers add to the kayak's strength. A large cockpit coaming rests on two deck side stringers.

Figure 9 illustrates the construction techniques looking into the cockpit. Analysis of the wooden framework proved it to be cedar. The bearded sealskin cover is crudely cleaned with the hair still attached in some places. Carrying handles are sewn into the ends.

Because of the generous rocker and deep V sec-tion, the Koryak kayak was initially very unstable, but highly maneuverable. The short waterline length and poorly finished outside cover would have made the craft slow. Satisfactory stability was obtained only through the use of "3 or 4 puds [108-143 lbs.] " rock ballast (Vdovin 1973:29). Any sea mammal caught by kayak would have had to be

Figure 8. Koryak kayak collected by Waldemar Jochelson around 1910. Length 8' 5.8". Collection Museum of Anthropology and Ethnography, Leningrad. MAE 956-49.

Figure 9. Inside view of the Koryak kayak detailed in Figure 8, looking forward in cockpit. Note wide plank used for a seat.

towed to shore because the craft is of such low volume that even a 150 pound seal would have the decks awash.

A distinctive feature of this kayak is the method of propulsion. Two short individual paddles were attached by lanyards to the cockpit coaming and presumably used together in the manner that a skier would double-pole.

One of the earliest descriptions of Koryak sea mammal hunting was written by the Russian scientist I. G. Voznesenskii in 1846 and quoted (in Russian) by Vdovin (1973:30). The description of the Karagintsy subgroup of Koryak people who lived around Karaginskiy Ostrov (Island) on the east coast of Kamchatka near latitude 58 degrees North:

> When an animal appears in the vicinity the Ukinets [the name Vosnesenskii gave the Karagintsy] lays down his paddle [double-bladed paddle], detaches the blades from the ends and uses them to paddle [stealthily] up to the animal. In stormy weather he uses an unequal-sided paddle and in calm weather, an even-bladed paddle. [I have not seen any of the double-bladed paddle specimens mentioned above] (Vdovin 1973:30).

V. V. Antropova, a Russian ethnographer with the Museum of Anthropology and Ethnography in Leningrad, reported that the Parentsy and Itkantsy Koryak used the single-bladed paddles. She also mentioned that the kayaker sealed himself into the cockpit by stretching his clothing over it (1971:34).

According to Antropova, the greatest hunting of sea mammals was among the Penzhina Koryaks — the Kamentsy, Parentsy and Itkantsy. Their spring hunting technique used the kayak as a support vessel for the larger baydar (umiak).

The men went hunting in several baydars, with 9 to 12 men to each baydar. Kayaks were also taken in addition to the baydars. The hunters' objective was to sail as close as possible to seals that were warming themselves or dozing on ice floes, without making any noise. Having sighted the game, one of the hunters would transfer from a baydar to a kayak and, attempting not to make any noise, he would sail [paddle?] up to the ice floe that was nearest the animal. Having gotten onto the ice floe, he would dart a harpoon. The tip of the harpoon upon striking the animal, detached itself from the pole. The wounded animal would begin to dive; this caused the line that joined the tip to the pole to unwind. The hunter would then sail up to the pole which was floating on the water, and gripping the end of the line, he would pull the game towards the baydar or would leave it on an ice floe where the hunters would later come to collect it (Antropova 1971:34).

Jochelson's report on the Koryaks' kayaking ability differs somewhat from Voznesenskii's. Jochelson commented, "The progress of the kayak in calm weather is extremely fast; but its use is not without danger, as it is easily upset by wind and waves, and it is necessary to balance it carefully while paddling. In stormy weather the Koryak do not venture upon the sea in kayaks" (1908:540).

The final comment on the Koryak kayak is from world traveler G. H. von Langsdorff who noted that the Koryak collected sea fowl eggs from some offshore islands.

> It is incomprehensible how people for the sake of a few eggs can trust themselves out at sea in such wretched canoes as they build; their lives are in manifest danger at every moment. Perhaps it is still more incomprehensible that they do not endeavour to construct boats of a better kind (von Langsdorff 1814:324).

Chukchi

The Chukchi occupied both coastal and inland areas of the Chukotka Peninsula. They used two kayak types, one in the maritime areas on the Arctic Ocean side of Chukotka and another inland in the Anadyr River area.

Two maritime-type Chukchi kayaks are preserved in the Ethnographic Museum of Sweden in Stockholm. A. E. Nordenskiold, who collected them on the north coast of Chukotka in 1879-1880, barely mentioned them in his 1881

two-volume publication. Figure 10 illustrates one of them. Nordenskiold noted that *"One seldom sees anatkuat, or boats intended for only one man..."* (1881 Vol. 1:94). While these maritime kayaks are similar to the inland types, they are rather strange in that they have no coamings for protection from the sea.

At the turn of the century, the ethnographer Waldemar Bogoras saw none of the maritime kayaks. He was told that they were *"...of various*

Figure 10. Lines and construction drawings of a maritime Chukchi kayak. Length 15' 2.2". Ethnographic Museum of Sweden, Stockholm. Sheet (1 of 1). Line drawing IV-G-1M © Canadian Museum of Civilization.

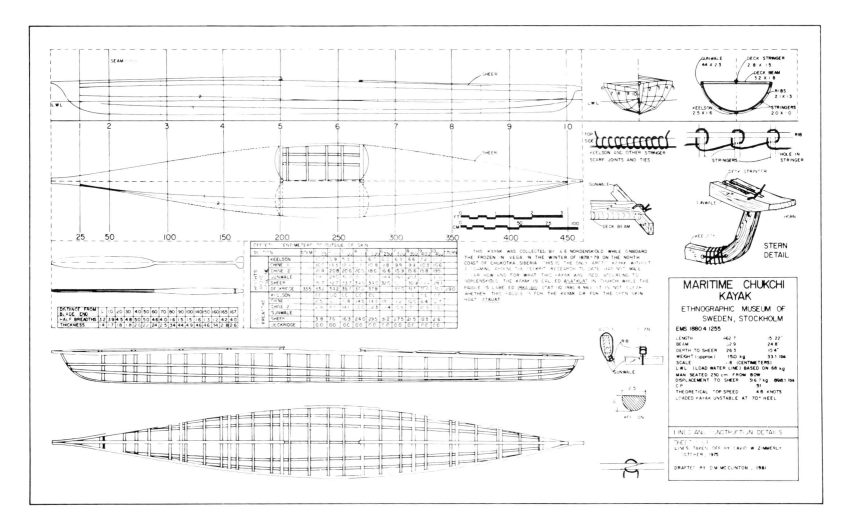

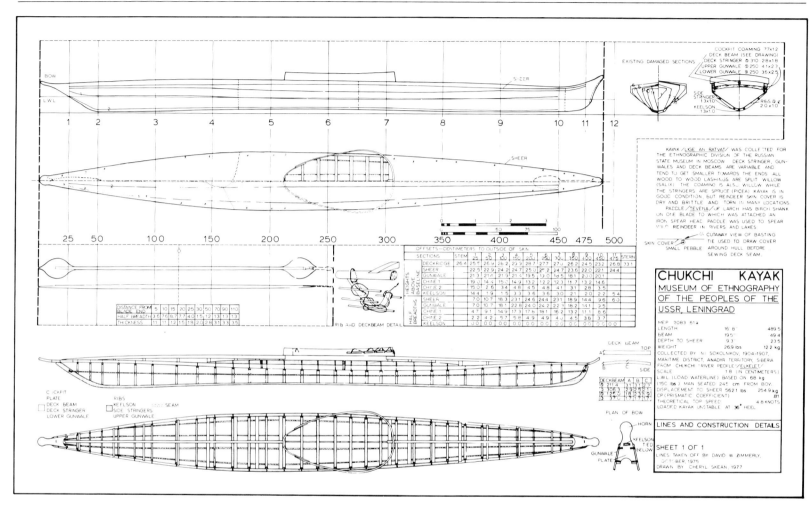

Figure 11. Lines and construction drawings of a reindeer Chukchi kayak (inland kayak). Length 16' 8". Museum of Ethnography, Leningrad. Sheet (1 of 1). Line drawing IV-G-2M © Canadian Museum of Civilization.

sizes, sometimes have two seats, and are used for seal-hunting and travel, as mentioned many times in Chukchee tales" (1909:121).

According to Antropova, only the inland type of Chukchi kayak survived to the end of the nineteenth century "...among those groups of Chukchi who combined reindeer herding with fishing and hunting" (1961:19). She mentioned that the inland kayak "...was used mainly for hunting wild deer during their annual river crossings. This took place along the Anadyr and several other rivers of the

Chukchi Peninsula. The river kayak was usually covered with reindeer skins, and the cockpit opening was larger than that of the kayaks of the coastal population" (p. 19).

Figure 11 illustrates a specimen of the inland type of kayak collected between 1904 and 1907 by N. I. Sokolnikov. This kayak is preserved in Leningrad's Museum of the Peoples of the USSR.

The plan view of the kayak as shown in Figure 11 looks very modern with the greatest beam forward of the cockpit and a shape not unlike the delta outline of a racing kayak. With a narrow beam of 19.5'' and a rounded V-bottom, this kayak would require skillful handling to remain upright, but could be very fast. The slight reverse rocker seen in the drawings may be the result of crowded museum storage conditions, but in any case it would straighten out with the weight of a paddler.

This frame is lightly built and with the reindeer skin cover weighs just under 27 pounds. The long double-bladed paddle with short wide blade ends had a spear point fitted on one end. This enabled a paddler to spear a reindeer and then maneuver the craft quickly out of the way. The cockpit is long and "... *remains open, because there is no need of making it water-tight for use on the river*" (Bogoras 1909:135).

Siberian Eskimo

The Siberian or Asiatic Eskimo lived on the coastal area of East Cape, Siberia and on Big Diomede Island in the Bering Strait. Very little is known about the kayak of the Siberian Eskimo. As far as I know there are no specimens anywhere.

Figure 12. Drawing of a Siberian Eskimo kayak said to be like that of the maritime Chukchi (from Bogoras's *The Chukchee*, 1909, Fig. 47c, p. 135).

The drawing in Figure 12 was made from a photograph shot by Bogoras in the Eskimo village of Wute'en. He said only that it was about 15 feet long. He collected a model of a kayak made at Indian Point in Siberia. The absence of kayaks among Siberian Eskimos is puzzling.

The noted Russian linguist G. A. Menovshchikov said that:

> *The displacement of the kayak by the canoe among the Eskimos of Asia which was completed during the first quarter of the 20th century is accounted for by the predominance among the latter of group hunting of large sea animals — whales and walrus, and also by the fact that the use of the kayak under the always open and stormy conditions of the Bering Sea was more difficult and dangerous than putting to sea in a kayak in the sheltered fiords of Greenland or the straits of the Canadian archipelago (1959:53).*

But it was just as stormy on the Alaska side of Bering Strait and all the people there had kayaks. Other forces may have been at work to cause the disappearance of the kayak. The Eskimos on nearby St. Lawrence Island in Alaska are linguistically and culturally closely related to the Siberian Eskimos. At the time of European contact, models found in archaeological sites were the only evidence of kayak use on St. Lawrence Island. The disappearance of the kayak among the two groups remains a mystery.

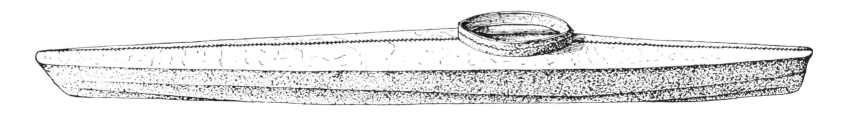

Figure 13. Lithograph of one-hole and two-hole Aleut kayaks drawn by Louis Choris, explorer artist with the voyage of Otto von Kotzebue in 1816. Collection Alaska State Museum. V-A-478.

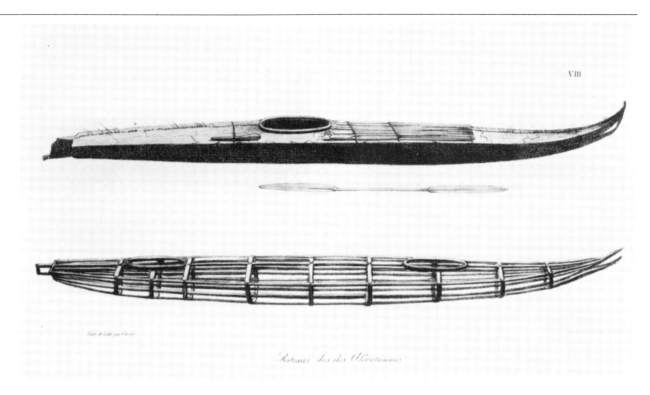

Bateaux des îles Aléoutiennes

The island-dwelling Aleut usually had open water all year long and depended heavily upon the sea for their livelihood. Two thousand years before the Christian era, the Aleut "...had a very robust, complex kayak hunting culture" (Aigner 1974:11). Thus their one-hole baidarka probably represents up to 5,000 years of development and evolution and is the ultimate in sea kayak design.

The Aleutian Islands were first discovered by Europeans in 1741 when Vitus Bering was returning to Kamchatka from the American shores. *"When in 1742 the fellow travelers of Bering returned to*

Kamchatka, they brought with them a large quantity of sea-otter's skins. This evoked a long series of merchants' and hunters' expeditions to the east, and thus the whole chain of the Aleutian Islands between Kamchatka and the Alaska Peninsula was discovered" (Jochelson 1933:2).

The Russian traders were eager to procure sea otter skins for the lucrative trade in China. They subjugated and organized the Aleut into fleets of two-man kayak teams coordinated by a leader in a

Figure 14. Two-hole Aleut kayak, probably collected prior of the turn of the century. The bow structure has apparently been modified and the walrus skin covering is not of traditional Aleut quality. Length 20'7". Collection Sheldon Jackson Museum. III.X.20

Photograph by Mark Daughhetee

Figure 15. One-hole Aleut baidarka (kayak) from a drawing by John Webber, Captain Cook's shipboard artist during the 1778 voyage to the Aleutian Islands.

Figure 16. Lines and construction drawings of a one-hole Aleut kayak (baidarka) collected on Akun Island in the Aleutian Islands in 1845 by the Russian explorer I. G. Voznesenskii. Length 19′ 1″. Museum of Anthropology, Leningrad. Sheet (1 of 1). Line drawing IV-F-5M © Canadian Museum of Civilization.

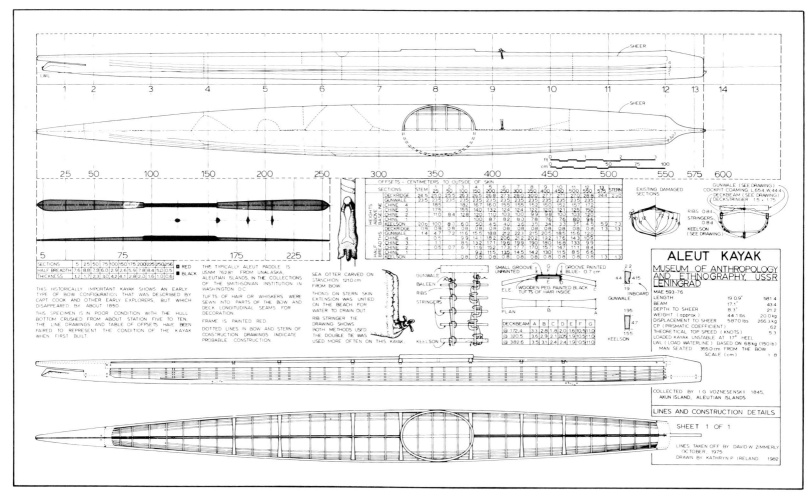

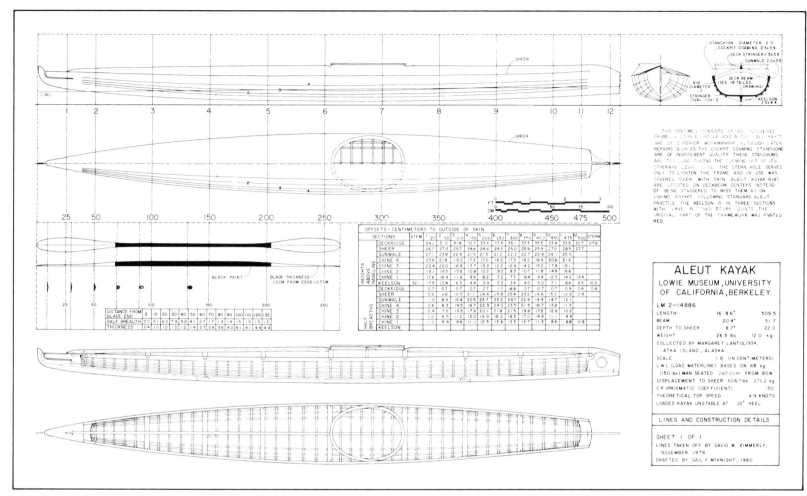

Figure 17. Lines and construction drawings of a one-hole Aleut kayak, collected on Atka Island in 1934 by anthropologist Margaret Lantis. Length 16' 8.6". University of California, Lowie Museum. Sheet (1 of 1). Line drawing IV-F-1M © Canadian Museum of Civilization.

three-hole kayak. These efficient and deadly work groups were shipped from Alaska to Baja California, almost completely exterminating the sea otters.

Today the Aleut do not use kayaks. According to Robert-Lamblin, "Its disappearance seems to be linked partially to the extermination of the fur-bearing animals whose skins were used to cover the kayaks, and partially to the final prohibition of the sea otter hunt after 1911..." (1980:6).

One-hole Kayak

Before the Russians came, the Aleut did most of their hunting and travelling in one-hole baidarkas similar to the one in Figure 15. This was the type of kayak seen in Unalaska in 1778 by Captain Cook. The distinctive forked bow shape was said by Cook "to catch hold of everything that comes in the way; to prevent which, they fix a piece of small stick from point to point" (1785:514). One kayak I examined in Leningrad had a piece of twisted baleen joining these points.

Bow Shape

This bow shape may well have represented an animal. One of Robert-Lamblin's informants stated that it "...*represents an otter swimming on its back, the anterior portion of the fork representing the head and the other portion the animal's forelegs*" (1980:18). According to another informant, "...*the entire stempost represents the head of an otter with its mouth open*" (p. 18).

In 1802 Sauer described the bow shape as fish-like in profile.

> *The head of the boat is double the lower part, sharp, and the upper part flat, resembling the open mouth of a fish, but contrived thus to keep the head from sinking too deep in the water... (Sauer 1802:159).*

Photograph by Mark Daughhetee

Sauer's statement is the only source that suggests the functional reason for the bifid or two-part bow on Aleut kayaks. It allowed the bottom portion to be sharp and narrow like a cutwater, while the upper part was large and triangular in shape to give more buoyancy. This made the bow concave in cross section, a configuration that would be otherwise impossible to achieve with skin and wood.

The Aleut kayak described by Cook was only 12 feet long. I have calculated that the average length of one-hole Aleut baidarkas is 17 feet 5 inches with an average beam of 19.3 inches and a weight of just over 35 lbs. The workmanship on most Aleut kayaks is superb. Special decorations inside on the deck beams or on a forward stanchion were related to the owner's helping spirit.

These Aleut vessels are perhaps the finest sea kayaks ever made by any Arctic peoples, being fast, light and seaworthy. Their perfection was commented on by several early explorers.

> *It seems to me that the Aleut baidarka is so perfect in its way that a mathematician himself could hardly add anything to the perfection of its sea going qualities (Veniaminov 1840:222).*

> *The baidars, or boats, of Oonalashka, are infinitely superior to those of any other island.*

Figure 19. Aleut two-hole kayak model with figures. Kayak is decorated with tufts of hair. Figures have wooden hunting hats and gut parkas. Length 15". Collection Alaska State Museum. II-F-168.

Figure 18. Carved wooden sea otter attached to stanchion in one-hole Aleut baidarka collected in 1845. Collection Museum of Anthropology and Ethnography. MAE 593-76.

If perfect symmetry, smoothness, and proportion, constitute beauty, they are beautiful; to me they appeared so beyond anything that I ever beheld. I have seen some of them as transparent as oiled paper, through which you could trace every formation of the inside, and the manner of the natives' sitting in it; whose light dress, painted and plumed bonnet, together with his perfect ease and activi-

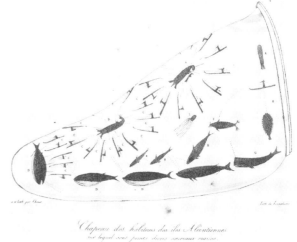

Chapeau des habitans des iles Aleutiennes

Figure 21. Drawing of an Aleut wooden hunting hat with various kayak hunting scenes painted on it. Colored lithograph by Louis Choris, from his Voyage pittoresque autour du monde, 1822. Collection Alaska State Museum. V-A-476.

ty, added infinitely to its elegance. Their first appearance struck me with amazement beyond expression (Sauer 1802:157).

Kayak Hats

The Aleut were known for their decorated wooden-peaked hats, used to protect their eyes from salt spray when kayaking. The hats could cause problems.

In a strong wind the large caps can cause the destruction of an unexperienced rider, because the wind can very easily catch under the cap and by its strength overturn his baidarka. Therefore, at such a time many remove them as a measure of protection (Veniaminov 1840:218-19).

Robert-Lamblin reported that in trading, a kayak hat was "... worth one to three slaves..." (1980:12).

Kayak Construction

One whole year and more is spent in building such a small boat, on which account they prefer purchasing it at a dear rate. The bare collecting together as much wood on the shore as is requisite for a baidar, is attended with infinite toil and trouble (Sarycev [1802, English edition 1807, II, 73] quoted in Hrdlicka 1945:123).

Most of the kayak frame and the paddle were made from black spruce. Yellow cedar was used for the ribs, cockpit coaming and spear thrower because of its strength, lightness and good bending characteristics. Red cedar was a favorite for the harpoon shaft, bailer and knife holder. (Robert-Lamblin 1980:18)

Framework

Veniaminov reported that *"The keel is always in three pieces in order that the baidarka may have movement when on the run or, as they say, that it may 'bend' over the wave"* (1840:222-23).

Also according to Veniaminov, the greatest beam of a baidarka is near the bow (Ibid. p.223). Margaret Lantis noted that there was *"...considerable variation in the framework..."* (1933-34:112). One of her informants insisted that the design of the central section was all-important for good handling characteristics (Ibid. p. 112).

The kayak frame was lashed together with sea lion sinew cord and painted with a blood and powdered red mineral mixture.

Skin Cover

Lantis' informants reported that two sealskins and one sea lion skin were used to cover the kayak with the sea lion in the midsection. Decorative tufts of sea lion hair were sewn into the central deck seam. *"Two flaps of skin were allowed to protrude from the median seam behind the hatch. A hole was made thru each so that a cooking pot could be tied to one and a tea kettle to the other one"* (Lantis 1933-34:115).

Waterproofing

The skin cover was waterproofed about once a month with boiled seal oil. This also made the cover *"translucent enough to reveal the framework within or to allow a passenger lying inside the kayak to see the reflections of the water quite clearly"* (Robert-Lamblin 1980:10-11).

Figure 22. Aleut sea otter hunters with their two-hole kayaks pulled up on the beach at Belkofsky Island, probably early 1900s. Note the gun cases strapped to the foredecks, the drying kamleikas (gutskin raincoats), and spray skirts held up with sticks to prevent water from entering the boats. Photograph courtesy of the University of Washington Instructional Media Production Services.

Figure 23. Aleut three-hole kayak model with wood figures in painted hunting hats and gut parkas. Model is of skin stretched over wood frame. Length 20.75". Collection Alaska State Museum. II-F-166.

Figure 24. Lines and construction drawings of a two-hole Aleut kayak (baidarka) collected on Unalaska Island in the Aleutian Islands in 1889. Length 20' 7". U.S. National Museum, Washington, D.C. Sheet (1 of 1). Line drawing IV-F-4M © Canadian Museum of Civilization.

Two & Three-hole Kayaks

The two-hole kayaks had an average length of 20 feet 8 inches with a beam of 23.2 inches.

Veniaminov said that:

The two-hatched baidarka was always in use among the Aleuts but only for the transfer of light freight or for riding on the sea of an old man with a child, but even up to the present day, there has never been an instance of two

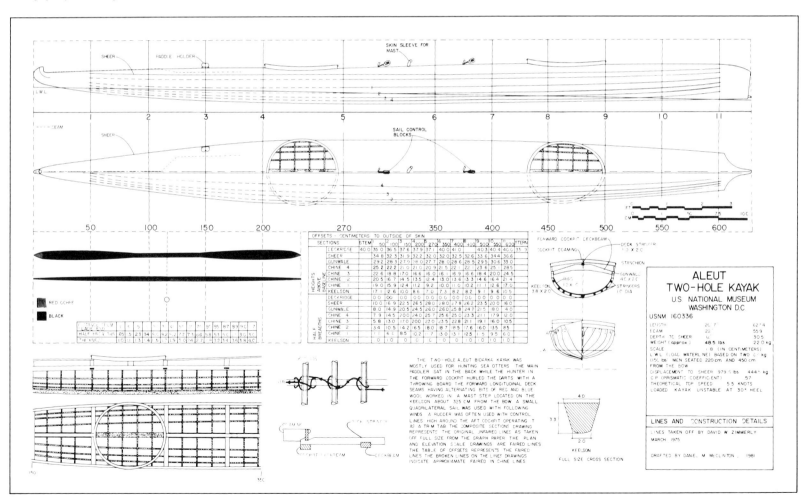

young and healthy rowers of their own will riding out in hunt of the otter in a two-hatched boat. This was regarded as shameful (Veniaminov 1840:222).

Three-hole kayaks were said to be an invention of the Russians used to transport traders, explorers and missionaries and goods in the central cockpit. The average length of these kayaks was 24 feet 8 inches with a beam of 28 inches.

Figure 25. Two-hole and three-hole baidarkas at Unalaska. Note how bowman in two-hole craft is hurling the dart while the sternman balances. In the three-hole baidarka, the bowman is using a rifle while middleman and sternman balance. Photograph from early 1900s, courtesy of the U.S. National Archives.

Kayak Use

The major use of the Aleut baidarkas was for hunting sea mammals. After the Russians came, the hunting emphasis was on sea otters.

Sea Otter Hunting

Jochelson described the use of the throwing dart which was the main hunting weapon in use by the Aleut.

Speed Secrets

A number of writers have commented on special bone joints that were secret construction practices known to few kayak builders. Von Langsdorff was one of the first writers to note these joints.

In some places, where the different pieces of the skeleton are fastened together, two flat bones are bound cross-ways over the joint in the inside, and this the chief assured me was of the greatest use in stormy weather. As the fastenings are apt to be loosened by the shock of the waves, these bones contribute essentially towards preventing such an inconvenience; but this art is not known to all, and is kept very much a secret by those who possess it (von Langsdorff 1814:42).

Figure 26. Bone strips used at deck beam/deck stringer junctures to reduce friction and allow joint to "work" in a seaway. Photographs and research courtesy of Joseph Lubischer.

Figure 27. Bone strips used at deck beam/deck stringer junctures to reduce friction and allow joint to "work" in a seaway. Deck stringer has been turned up 90 degrees from normal for a better view of the bone strips.

These joints were not seen on museum kayak specimens. Recently however, Joseph Lubischer discovered bone strips and ball joints on kayak pieces in the Thomas Burke Memorial Washington State Museum at the University of Washington. The pieces were included with a kayak frame collected in 1920 from Dutch Harbor(Unalaska).

Veniaminov also commented about the bone joints.

In the best one-hatched baidarka, in order to give them speed, they inserted as many as 60 small bones in all the joints; the bones were used as plugs [vtulochka], the end of the axis [vertliug], the locks [zamochek], plates [plastinka], etc. When such a baidarka was in motion, almost every part was in movement. But at the present time no one has these small bones and no one, save for the oldsters, knows how to make them or to use them as necessary. (I had a three-hatched baidarka with small bones, but it was not at all better than a plain one.) (Veniaminov 1840:220).

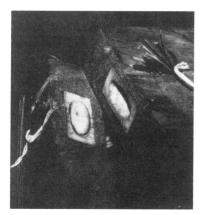

Figure 28. Carved bone ball and socket in stern crosspiece.

Figure 29. Carved bone ball and socket in keelson scarf joint.

The final comment on the bone joints comes from the 1933-34 field notes of anthropologist Margaret Lantis.

A groove was made in the keel of the bidarka with a piece of bone fitting over it and in the groove an ivory ball was placed. This ball moved back and forth in its groove on the principle of a ball-bearing, to increase speed [Makary Zaochney] (Lantis 1933-34:113).

The small rectangular piece of bone ... was found by one of the [children] on the beach [and] was used in the bidarka. It was fitted into a groove in the keel on the inside of the bidarka and moved along this groove. Only one such device was used in a bidarka. We could not get a precise explanation but [apparently] it was used to prevent strain and rubbing by the ribs. No lines were attached to it. (Lantis 1933-34:114).

...while throwing a dart with the right hand the boatsman kept the skin-boat in equilibrium by putting the paddle across the boat and pressing it against the railing with the left hand (1933:55). [Jochelson was on the Aleutians from 1909-1910, just before sea otter hunting was banned.]

Weapons alone were not sufficient for hunting the sea otter.

...the Aleuts believed that the sea-otter was a transformed human being, they endeavored to ornament their bidarkas, their garments, and their spears as much as possible, in the belief that the sea-otter would be attracted by the beauty of the outfit (Petroff 1884:155).

Figure 30. Drawing by Henry Elliott (*Our Arctic Province*, 1886) showing surround method used by a group of two-hole Aleut kayaks to hunt sea otters. The kayakers in the middle have raised a paddle to signal that the sea otter dived underwater. Collection Alaska Historical Library.

Veniaminov described a sea otter hunt in detail.

Having selected a very calm day, at daybreak, after having first inspected the shores, the hunters set off to sea to search for otters in certain localities. On the sea all the baidarki go in a line or formation at such a distance from one another that it would be

possible to see an otter between them. In a
large party this line is stretched out for
several versts (1 verst = .66 mile). The
hunter, who first sees the otter, or to whose
baidarka the otter is closest, makes a signal
by holding up his oar; he holds it thus, until
the other baidarki have encircled him, or
until the otter appears in another spot. Immediately upon seeing the signal, either one
detachment of the party, that is, several
baidarki, or sometimes the whole party encircle the spot where the otter was first seen,
forming a circle, as nearly as possible, and
holding their javelins ready. The otter, seeing
the enemy, does not immediately dive into
the water, but examines and considers all the
circumstances, and he performs various
maneuvers and tricks in the water in order to
escape from danger. But no matter how long
he may remain in the water, he must finally
appear on the surface of the sea. And the
hunter near whom the otter appears, [344] if
he can, flings a javelin at the otter and immediately raises his oar; the other baidarki
again encircle him, but now at a smaller
distance because the otter, the second time,
cannot go far and remain long in the water.
And this is done until a javelin finds its mark
in the otter. The otter which has been
wounded can be considered to have been
caught because the javelin, dragging after
him in the water, slows down his
movements, and even if he should want to
hide when he emerges from the water the
javelin reveals the place where he is.

After the first javelin they fling a second and
a third and even more. But the otter always
belongs to the one who flung the first javelin
which found its mark. If two or more struck
the animal at once, the otter goes to the one
whose javelin is closest to the head
(Veniaminov 1840:342-44).

**Figure 31. Elliott drawing showing Unalaska kayakers
hunting humpback whales. Fig. 31 and 32 collection
Alaska Historical Library.**

Fishing

Kayaks were also used for halibut and cod fishing.

**Figure 32. Elliott drawing showing Unalaska kayaker
fishing for cod.**

Figure 33. Elliott drawing showing cooperative method used by a one-hole and a two-hole kayak to catch large halibut, using paddles for stability. The man in the one-hole kayak will kill the halibut with a specially designed club. Collection Alaska Historical Library.

Warfare

The Aleut were reported to engage in great sea battles with their baidarkas.

The Aleuts also engaged in sea battles but very rarely and almost exclusively on the occasion of an unexpected encounter with the foe. But the Aleuts, enjoying a superiority over the men of Kadiak because of the greater speed of their baidarki, sought to search them out on the sea. When they met an enemy on the sea, they did not attack at once, but first they made inroads upon them, shooting arrows. They pursued him until they saw that the foe was weakening. Then, suddenly and with fury they attacked and sank the boats of the enemy without mercy until the conquered begged for peace. Maritime warfare brought them no gain, except glory...(Veniaminov 1840:104).

Paddles and Paddling Techniques

Double-bladed paddles were standard, but single-bladed ones were carried as spares on deck. The Aleut baidarka is easy to right after a capsize although the techniques for doing so were never recorded. Sarycev reported in 1802 that:

Mears says in his travels, that the Aleutians could turn themselves over in their baidars, and regain their position at pleasure; but this is not the case. Whenever they are so unfortunate as to be overturned, their death is inevitable, if no one be at hand to assist them... (Sarycev [1802 English edition 1807, II, 73] quoted in Hrdlicka 1945:123)

Veniaminov, however, implied that capsize recovery techniques were known.

Thus, today there are extremely few, if any, of the former riders who, when their boats capsized, could set them right side up by themselves and take their seats in them, or who could set ... upright with a skillful motion of the oar without emerging from the baidarka (Veniaminov 1840:73-74).

Ballast

The light, narrow one-hole kayak was very tender without any load. Stability was enhanced through the addition of stone ballast. Jochelson said that the ballast amounted to about:

...25 kilograms [55 pounds], distributed in the middle, stern and prow, to prevent the boat from capsizing. It is regarded as a sin to throw the ballast into the sea. The stones must be brought to land from where they were taken, otherwise the boatsman, it is

*believed, will be drowned. Even when the
load of the skin-boat becomes too heavy from
the returns of fishing or hunting, the stones
have to be brought to the shore (Jochelson
1933:55).*

Kayak Rudder, Mast and Sail

After the arrival of Europeans, two-hole kayaks and
occasionally one-hole ones were provided with a
rudder, mast and square sail. Lantis noted that the
mast was placed between the two hatches, but
nearer to the foreward one. *"The rudder was
manipulated by ropes by the man in the foreward
hatch while the man in the rear hatch paddled"*
(1933-34:95).

Navigation

Margaret Lantis is the only writer to describe Aleut
methods of navigation.

*The Aleuts had no charts, maps, diagrams of
any kind. Practically every island was inhabited in the old days so that if men were
travelling in a certain area for the first time,
they could ask their way from island to
island. They travelled at night as well as in
the daytime, guiding by stars and moon. They
also watched the winds, tide rips, etc. Con-
stantine [Margaret Lantis' informant] had
crossed the pass between Amlia and Atka in
heavy fog, taking his direction from the ocean
swell (Lantis 1933-34:99).*

*The customary mode of travel ... was for 8
bidarkas to travel together, spread out in a
long line at right angles to the direction of
advance. If one man sighted the island which
they were seeking, he would yell and all
would close in (Ibid. p. 95).*

**Figure 34. "Man and woman of Oonalashka." Hand-
colored engraving. The man is shown in kayaking gear.
The depiction of a dog in this context is unusual. Collection Alaska State Museum.**

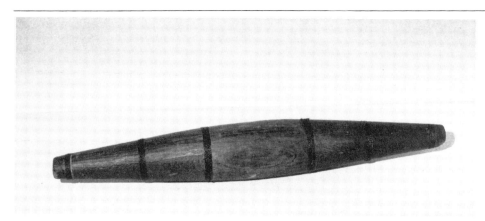

Figure 35. Wooden bailer used to pour off any water that collected in the kayak. Water was sucked into the tube, a finger placed over the bottom hole and the water was then emptied over the side. Unalaska, 1978.

Figure 36. Aleut two-hole kayak model with wood figures and hunting equipment. Length 15". Collection Alaska State Museum. II-F-171.

Damage Control

Inflated seal throats or bladders were used for damage control. Veniaminov described their use.

In the number of things indispensable to the baidarka, formerly belonged the bladder, i.e. the cleaned stomach of a seal or sea-lion, which was needed for the occasion when a rider overturned. In such a situation, to emerge from the baidarka and set it on its keel again without shipping water, and, even if water pours in, to bail it out, is not very difficult. But to get into the baidarka without any other point of support is completely impossible. An inflated bladder on such an occasion was extremely useful, because with its assistance the rider could maintain himself on the water and get into the baidarka. It would happen that if the sheathing of the baidarka should somehow be torn, the rider with the assistance of the bladder got out of the baidarka, turned it over, and repaired it, and then got into it again, if this took place in calm weather. In a brisk wind and under unfavorable circumstances, they placed the bladder in the baidarka, and there inflated it as much as possible. It supported the baidarka on the surface of the water, notwithstanding the fact that it was full of water (Veniaminov 1840:225-26).

Cultural Context of the Kayak

Being central to Aleut culture, education in its use began at an early age.

The process of learning to paddle and hunt in a kayak began very early in the life of an Aleut boy: by the age of 6-8. Under the guidance of an experienced hunter — his

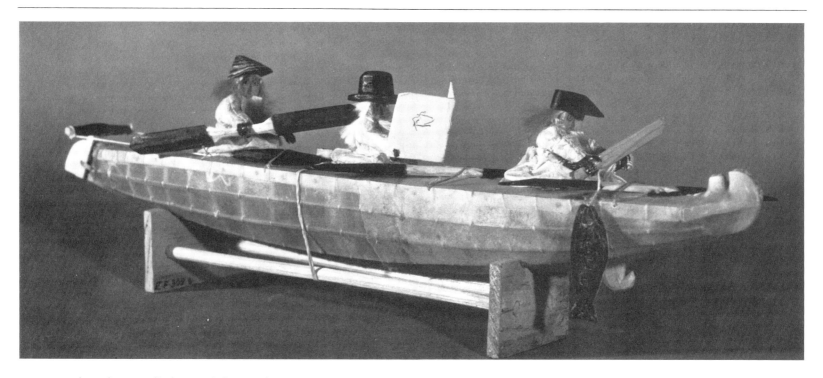

maternal uncle, grandfather or father — the boy would begin with physical training intended to develop the muscles of the back, neck, shoulders and arms, to train him to maintain a sitting position, with his legs extended, for ever longer periods ... and to harden him to the cold by having him bathe every day in the sea. The child also practiced shooting at a target, so that later he would be able to harpoon game.

As an adolescent, the would-be hunter continued his training in a two-man kayak; at this time he learned to launch and land the kayak, to paddle against the current, to right the kayak with his paddle if it capsized, to repair damage, to recognize game and to approach it, etc. (Robert-Lamblin 1980:12).

The kayak was important in another context.

... in the Aleut oral tradition, the kayak is not an object; it is a living being, male, a hunting partner which attempts to identify itself with its master and would like to share his married life. Their fates, indeed, are bound up together, and their lives end at the same time: they disappear at sea together or, on land, share the same grave (Robert-Lamblin 1980:12).

Figure 37. Aleut three-hole kayak model with figures. The center figure represents a Russian priest holding a Bible. Model is skin stretched over wooden frame. Made by Sergie Sovoroff of Nikolski, Alaska. Length 17.75''. Collection Alaska State Museum. II-F-309.

The term Pacific Eskimo is used for the Kodiak (Koniag) Eskimo of the Kodiak Island area and for the Chugach Eskimo of Prince William Sound.

Figure 38. Lines and construction details of a Kodiak one-hole kayak collected in 1851 by Heinrich J. Holmberg on Kodiak Island. Length 14' 2.9" by 25.9". Danish National Museum, Copenhagen. Sheet (1 of 1). Line drawing IV-E-25M © Canadian Museum of Civilization.

Kayak Construction

The Pacific Eskimo kayaks and people are often confused with Aleut kayaks and people because the Russians tended not to distinguish between the two groups. Dorothy Jean Ray noted that this "...confusion has been compounded by the fact that the Russians also called the true Koniag and Chugach Eskimos 'Aleuts,' a name that some of the Koniag and Chugach descendants have retained to this day" (1981:15).

However, the kayaks, or baidarkas, of the Aleut and Pacific Eskimo had several distinctive differences.

The Pacific Eskimo kayak was more heavily built, had a greater beam and the gunwales came together in a point at the stern instead of to a crosspiece as on the Aleut kayak. Ribs were let

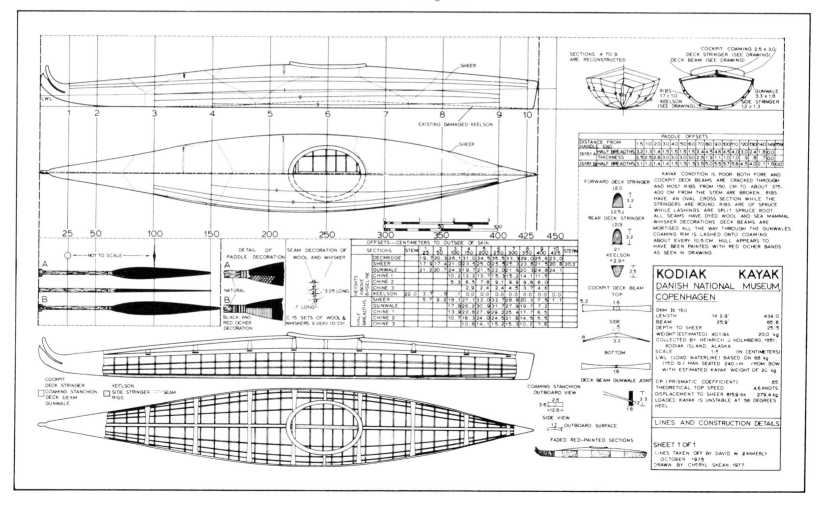

into the underside of the gunwales, carefully avoiding any location where there was a deck beam.

Like the Aleut, the Pacific Eskimo had one-, two- and three-hole kayaks, but it is problematic whether the three-hole variety existed before Europeans. Not enough specimens of the Koniag and Chugach kayaks survive to tell if there were any major differences in design and construction among their several varieties.

Kodiak Eskimo

Russian Explorer Urey Lisiansky made much use of Pacific Eskimo baidarkas. In 1814 he wrote:

...the Cadiack men deserve great credit for the invention of the bidarka, which is lightly constructed of wood, fastened together with whalebone, and covered over with seal-skins, the seams of which are so well sewed that not a drop of water can get through.... The bidarkas paddle very fast, and are safer at sea in bad weather than European boats; especially when provided with good hatchway cloths, which are always drawn over holes, answering to hatchways, and extend around the waists of the people sitting in them... When there are several of these vessels in company, and a storm overtakes them, they fasten together in parties of three or four, and thus ride it out, like so many ducks tossed up and down by the waves, without the smallest danger. At first I disliked these leathern canoes on account of their bending elasticity in the water, arising from their being slenderly built; but when accustomed to them, I thought it rather pleasant than otherwise (Lisiansky 1814:211-12).

One-hole Kodiak Kayak

Figure 38 shows a typical one-hole Kodiak kayak. It is rather beamy for its length, but makes an excellent seaworthy and seakindly craft. It is capable of carrying a good load inside and with a paddler is stable up to 56 degrees of heel.

Figure 39. Single-hole Pacific Eskimo kayak, 1888. Photograph from the U.S.S. Thetis collection, courtesy of the Alaska Historical Library.

Figure 40. Two two-hole and one three-hole Pacific Eskimo kayaks. Photograph courtesy of the Anchorage Museum of History and Art.

Three-hole Kodiak Kayak

Figure 41. Inside view of three-hole Kodiak kayak towards the bow.

Figure 42a. Lines and construction details of a three-hole Kodiak Eskimo kayak collected in 1805 by Russian explorer Urey Lisiansky. Length 26' 5.7". Museum of Anthropology, Leningrad. Sheet (1 of 2). Line drawing IV-E-22M © Canadian Museum of Civilization.

The three-hole type of kayak was said by some early writers to have been introduced by the Russians. The requirement was for a locally manufactured craft that could be used to explore shallow rivers, to carry missionaries spreading 'The Word' (among other things) and to carry trade goods. The large middle cockpit held the Russian traveler and trade items while the smaller end cockpits were manned by native paddlers.

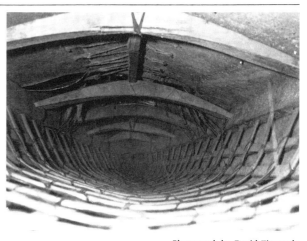

Photograph by David Zimmerly

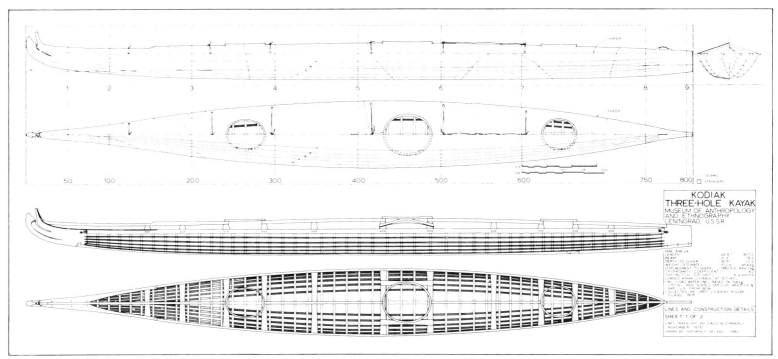

31

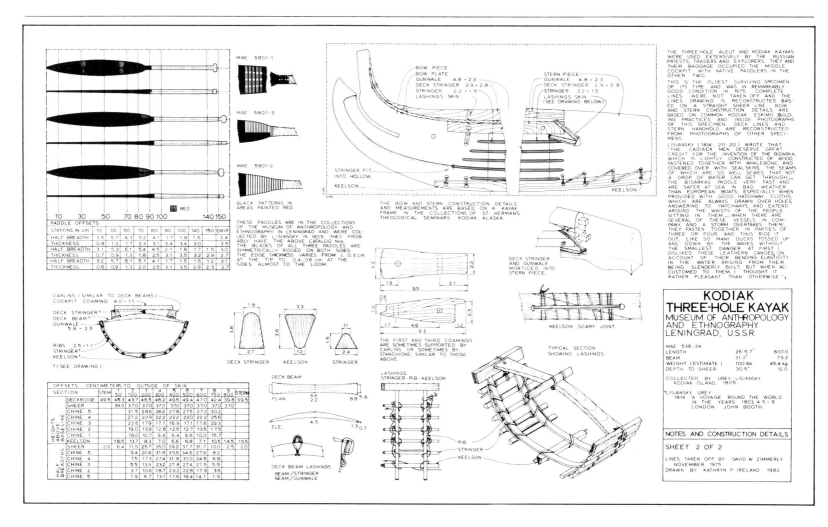

Figure 42 shows what may be the oldest surviving Alaskan baidarka anywhere. It is a three-hole Kodiak kayak (baidarka) in Leningrad's Museum of Anthropology and Ethnography. The kayak was collected (and probably used for exploration) in 1805 by the Russian explorer Urey Lisiansky.

Figure 41 is an inside view of the Leningrad kayak looking towards the bow. Some flattening out of the hull bottom has taken place because of insufficient bottom support. All parts of the kayak

frame are made from wood. The whalebone mentioned above in the Lisiansky quote actually refers to whale baleen, a fibrous plastic-looking material that was often used to lash the ribs to the stringers as in this photograph.

Figure 42b. Second sheet of lines and construction details of a three-hole Kodiak Eskimo kayak collected in 1805 by Russian explorer Urey Lisiansky. Length 26′ 5.7″. Museum of Anthropology, Leningrad. Sheet (2 of 2). Line drawing IV-E-22M © Canadian Museum of Civilization.

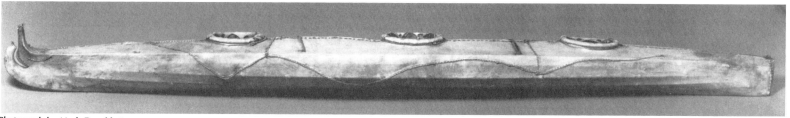

Figure 43. Three-hole Pacific Eskimo kayak model c.1900. Length 80". Loan collection, Alaska State Museum.

Kayak Use

All manner of sea mammals were hunted by the Pacific Eskimo including seals, sea otters and whales.

Sea Otter Hunting

The Russians assembled hunters in two-hole kayaks from all the settlements under their control for special hunting parties to hunt sea otter. Before 1800 these parties had over 800 kayaks (1600 hunters), but by 1799 this dropped to 500 and in 1804 only about 300 (Black 1977:97).

The Russian Orthodox Priest Father Gideon described sea otter hunting as it was practiced by a small group of hunters between 1804-1807.

Sea otters are hunted at the Tugidok island. The hunters depart in a party of from 8 to 15 two-hatch baidarkas and travel about 10 miles out to sea. The first man who sights the otters signals the others by lifting his oar. The others try to encircle the place at a distance within range of their darts. Only those who sit in the forward hatch throw the darts; those who sit in the rear hatch maneuver the baidarka. The sea otter belongs to the hunter who is the first to wound the animal (Black 1977:97).

Whale Hunting

Lisiansky noted that whaling was done from one-hole baidarkas.

A Cadiack whaler, in a single bidarka, attacks only small whales; and for this purpose he is provided with a harpoon, the spear of which is made of slate-stone, and so fixed into the handle, as to detach itself when the whale is struck (Lisiansky 1814:202)

Father Gideon also wrote about the techniques employed to hunt whales.

The Company assigns the best of the Kad'iak inhabitants to hunt whales — about 30 men, who hunt near Kad'iak and Afognak. They are dispatched into various bays, by twos and fours, depending on the suitability of the

Figure 44. Three-hole Pacific Eskimo kayak model with figures. Length 16.625". Collection Alaska State Museum. II-F-165.

place. The hunters go out singly, in one-hatch baidarkas, and choose yearling whales because their meat and fat are tastier and tender.

Once the hunter observes such an animal, he approaches to the distance of not more than three sazhen (1 sazhen = 7 feet) and tries to aim his dart under the side flipper (last, as it is called here) and then tries to evade with great skill the thrashing beast: the whale can crush the hunter's boat or the wave caused by the diving whale may overturn his baidarka (Black 1977:102).

Hunting was always hard work, but especially when pressed by the Russians to fill certain quotas. Sometimes the hunters never returned.

In 1800 members of the Tugidok party were sent out to sea in inclement weather by the Hunter Lopatin, in spite of their protests. Thirty-two baidarkas, that is, 64 men were lost (Black 1977:97).

Lisiansky said that for hunters who died naturally or whose remains could be brought back to the community, "...their arrows, spears, and harpoons, are generally buried; and the frame of a bidarka is placed over them" (1814:200).

There were a number of survival techniques that the Kodiak paddlers used at sea. Some of these were described by Lieutenant Davydov in 1803.

...if a storm breaks when they are far from shore, and they have no chance of reaching shelter, then they gather the baidarkas together in two and threes and ride out the storm. They try to come alongside each other so that the sides of the baidarkas do not touch, for it would be easy to chafe through the leather. No more than three gather together in case there is a large wave and

many of them are dashed together. If just one baidarka is caught in a storm, then two large inflated bladders are sometimes tied to its sides (Davydov 1977:203).

Figure 45. Three-hole Pacific Eskimo kayak photographed in 1914. Photograph courtesy of the University of Washington Instructional Media Production Services.

Paddles and Paddling Technique

Kodiak paddlers used single-bladed paddles almost exclusively. Double-bladed paddles were used by the Kodiak paddlers, but I did not find any in the Leningrad museum collections.

Most Arctic kayakers paddled sitting down with their legs stretched out in front of them, "...the Koniags, however, for the most part, row in a kneeling position by simply placing piles of grass under their knees" (Davydov 1977:203).

Travelling through shallow marshy country they used special poles with multi-fingered ends to pole themselves along.

Education

The self-image of a Kodiak male depended on his being a hunter. But, being a hunter was synonymous with owning a baidarka. One of the worst insults that could be hurled at any male was to say " 'Your father had no baidarka, he was not any kind of hunter...' " (Black 1977:97).

Consequently, boys worked at learning the skills necessary to be hunters as soon as possible. Father Gideon tells us that:

> Beginning at age 14 they are trained to travel in baidarkas: at first they sail during calm weather into the bays to catch fish or to chase birds with their darts. Beginning at age 16, they are taken by their fathers and other kinsmen as members of the sea otter hunting parties (Black 1977:95).

Figure 46. Covered and uncovered three-hole Chugach Eskimo kayaks on beach at Knicklick (Kiniklik), Prince William Sound, Alaska. Photograph taken before 1925 by Merle LaVoy, courtesy of the Smithsonian Institution National Anthropological Archives.

Chugach Eskimo

When English navigator James Cook first sailed into Prince William Sound in 1778, he was met by three men in two kayaks. Other explorers that followed mentioned only one and two hole kayaks, but in later years the Chugach Eskimo had three-hole kayaks.

Frederica de Laguna photographed a three-hole Chugach baidarka frame in Chenega, Alaska, in the early 1930s. She was of the opinion that three-hole kayaks were introduced to the Chugach Eskimo sometime after 1788 when Colnett "...sketched and described the Chugach 2-hole bidarka and noted also the one-man type" (1956:245). She also said the Colnett remarked that "...sometimes 2 men sat back to back in one manhole, or the extra passenger was stowed away inside" (p. 245).

Birket-Smith said that only three-hole kayaks remained in existence in Prince William Sound in the 1930s. Due to an economic crisis around 1930 these kayaks experienced a renaissance. Birket-Smith noticed, "...one specimen under construction. The price of a complete baidarka was $75, and even in former times but a few persons knew how to build them" (1953:46).

The three-hole Pacific Eskimo kayak, perhaps even more than the Aleut version, was the workhorse of the Russian explorers, traders and missionaries. It was a major factor in the European exploration and settling of Alaska.

Construction

Traditional construction of the frame used some materials and details seldom seen in kayaks.

> The frame of the baidarka was made of hemlock, whereas the stem and stern as well as the cross pieces were of spruce. The

reason for the difference in material is that hemlock does not crack or break so easily as spruce, which is more dry. The trees were felled with a stone adze — fire was not used — and the wood was split with stone adzes and wedges of tough, young spruce wood....

Inside the baidarka two short vertical props were placed, one in front and the other one behind the man-hole. The same places there were also cross pieces between the gunwales. Close to the stem and stern similar cross pieces were placed...

For the sheathing of a one-hole baidarka six large skins of spotted seal were necessary, for a two-hole baidarka nine, and for a three-hole twelve skins. Skins of young sea lions might also be used...

Every year the skin had to be smeared with lukewarm oil, the best for this purpose being shark-liver oil. The seams were not especially smeared (Birket-Smith 1953:46, 47).

Use

Birket-Smith said that formerly the two-hole baidarka "...was the common hunting craft, whereas the one-hole baidarka served in porpoise hunting, fishing and travelling only" (1953:45).

Accessories

Birket-Smith has given us some excellent descriptions of the Chugach Eskimo kayak hunting implements, kayak accessories and methods of storing them onboard.

Hunting Implements

In front of each man-hole, but rather far apart, were two cross straps under which the hunting implements were placed. On the right side, in front of the foremost hole, was the harpoon with the head pointing aft and the butt of the shaft resting in the cleft between the prow pieces. The bow was also on the right side, but inside the harpoon. On the left were the throwing board and the seal club. On the right side in front of the second hole the lance was placed with the head pointing forward, and inside that another bow and a wooden quiver filled with arrows; the opening of the quiver was forward. On the left side was the whaling lance, also with the head pointing forward (Birket-Smith 1953:47).

Figure 47. Family in a three-hole Pacific Eskimo kayak. Photograph courtesy of the Anchorage Museum of History and Art.

Anthropometric Measurements: Rule of Thumb

Before the metric and English measurement systems were invented, people devised other ways to measure linear distances. One method used by Arctic peoples involved using parts of the body (anthro = man, metric = measurement) since these parts did not change much by the time one was an adult.

The arm span was a common measurement used by people all over the world and is preserved in the English system of measurement as a fathom, equal to six feet. The Chugach baidarka builders used the armspan plus many other special measures. Birket-Smith recorded these special measurements.

The following means of measuring when constructing a baidarka were obtained from Stephan, the only man in Chenega who was yet able to build one without assistance:

Length from stem piece to the first man-hole: **one arm span.**

Diameter of the first man-hole: **one lower arm plus the hand.**

Distance between the rims of the first and third man-hole: **one arm span plus three finger widths plus one hand with outstretched thumb.**

Length of gunwale: **three arm spans plus one lower arm and hand plus one hand with outstretched fingers.**

Width of baidarka at the middle: **one arm including the hand.**

Length of stem piece: **one lower arm including the hand.**

Width of lower prow: **three to four fingers.**

Width of upper prow: **four finger widths.**

Length of cleft between prows: **two thumbs plus two hand widths with outstretched thumbs.**

Radius of curve of lower prow: **one hand span (between thumb and middle finger).**

Height of stern below the gunwale: **one hand span** (Birket-Smith 1953:47-8)

Bailer

The bailer used by the Chugach Eskimo is the same as that used by the Aleut.

The water that by and by penetrates into the interior of the boat is sucked up in a sort of siphon; then the lower hole is closed with a finger and the water drained out. The siphon is spindle-shaped and made of one piece of wood split lengthwise, hollowed out and again lashed together (Birket-Smith 1953:48).

Paddles and Paddling Technique

The Chugach Eskimo had double-bladed paddles but normally used a one-bladed variety. Birket-Smith described the latter.

It had a spear-shaped blade and a crutch handle at the end of the shaft. The paddler was kneeling and took two or three strokes on one side, then two or three on the other (1953:48).

Davydov also mentioned paddling while kneeling.

The Chugaches build in small benches and instead of a litter they fit wooden knee plates (wooden slats which cause calluses on their knees and ankles) (1977:203).

Birket-Smith claimed that:

...a skilled paddler wearing the sleeveless gutskin jacket tied around the coaming of the hole and below his armpits was ... able to turn over in it. If a single man turned over in a two- or three-hole baidarka, the empty holes were covered up with gutskin (1953:48).

This is the only reference I know that indicates Chugach Eskimo knowledge of capsize recovery techniques.

Figure 48. A catch of king salmon at Nushagak, Alaska. Note kayak on rack. The bow of a Pacific Eskimo style kayak can be seen behind the bow of the Bering Sea kayak in front. Photograph courtesy of the Anchorage Museum of History and Art.

The Bering Sea kayaks are found in the area from Bristol Bay in the south to Norton Sound in the north. Kayak subtypes exist for Bristol Bay, Nunivak Island/Hooper Bay and Norton Sound. The difference between the first two subtypes is minimal. The average measurements for all these types are shown in Figure 5, "Siberian and Alaskan Kayak Average Measurements."

Figure 49. Nunivak Island couple transporting household goods. Photograph courtesy of the Smithsonian Institution, National Anthropological Archives.

Figure 50. Lines and construction details of a Hooper Bay kayak made by Dick Bunyan in 1976. Length 15' 1.4". National Museums of Canada, Ottawa. Sheet (1 of 7). Line drawing IV-E-19M © Canadian Museum of Civilization.

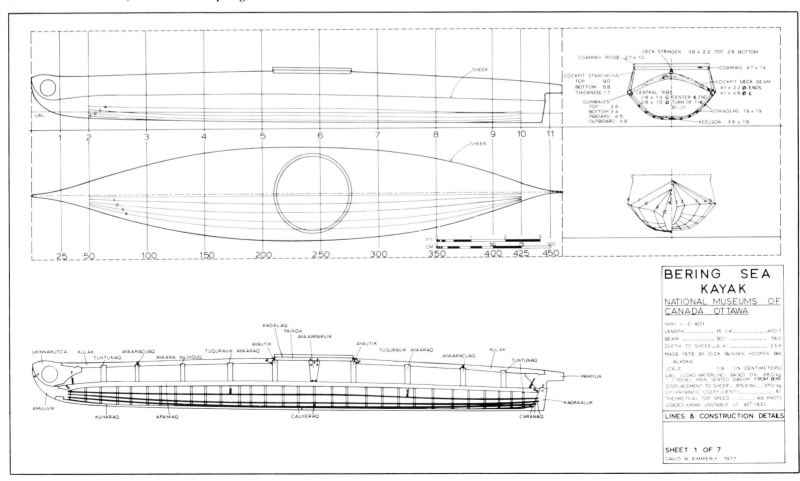

Nunivak/Hooper Bay

The kayak was the cornerstone of Eskimo society in the Yukon-Kuskokwim Delta area. Not only was it the means by which certain biological needs of the people were satisfied, it also was the basis among men for obtaining wealth and women. Anthropologist Margaret Lantis noted that wealth among the Nunivak Island Eskimo was a consequence of giving away goods, which depended on being a good hunter, which in turn depended on having a kayak and being a good kayaker (1946:158). A man could not get a wife if he were unable to support her, and without a kayak, support was impossible.

Kayak Building Ritual

The ritual surrounding the making of a kayak is indicative of its importance in the society. Curtis described the process in detail as he saw and heard it on Nunivak Island in 1927.

Their construction takes place with ceremony in the men's house, usually under the supervision of some old man well skilled in boat-making. The men measure and cut each individual part of the wooden frame according to a prescribed system based on the length of various members of the body or a combination of such members. Thus each man's kaiak is built according to the specifications of his own body and hence is peculiarly fitted to his use...

After each part is meticulously made according to measurement, the frame is put together with lashings of rawhide. The workmanship must of necessity be fine, because no cutting with edged tools may be done once the parts are finished and are being joined....

The night after the lashing of the kaiak frames is completed, the women gather to cut sealskins to size for the coverings, three thick and heavy hair-seal skins for the bottoms and sides, and two spotted-seal skins for the lighter decking. As they work, the women wear waterproof parkas, which are believed to prevent any evil influence from entering or afflicting the new kaiaks. ... The following day, while the women ... are sewing together the skins, the kaiak owners sit before the bows of the completed frames and sing their hunting songs in an almost inaudible tone, since these songs are both sacred and secret. Kaiak owners often have their sons beside them to learn these chants, which descend from father to son. After the singing, when the hides are nearly sewn, each wife brings to her husband a new wooden dish of fish or berries. Stripped to the waist, he throws a portion of the food to the floor as an offering, and prays for good luck during the coming hunting season....

Figure 51. Starboard cockpit coaming stanchion. This style of decoration was especially favored by Nunivak Islanders, but almost all such decorations related the starboard (right) side with good luck and maleness as represented by this smiling face. A frowning face on the port (left) side symbolized bad luck and femaleness. Roop Collection photograph of Nunivak kayak UM B-29, courtesy of the University Museum, Philadelphia.

As the last flap, on the after-deck, is sewn, after the frame is shoved into the completed covering, the now naked owner, accompanied by all the men present, sings his childbirth song to his new kaiak. The owner washes the cover with urine to remove any oil that may adhere to the surface, and rinses it in salt water. He then hauls his craft through the smoke-hole of the house and rests it in the snow, which will absorb dampness from its surface. Later he puts the kaiak on its rack and drapes over it his talismans, strung on belts, which are later to be kept in the kaiak....

On returning to the men's house, the owner dresses in new parka and boots, and, grasping a bunch of long grass fibres, makes motions of sweeping toward the entrance. By this action he brushes outside any evil influence or contamination from his kaiak, the covering which has been made by women (Curtis 1930:12,13,15).

Kayak Design

The Bering Sea kayaks were built with a broad and deep hull with rounded bilges and a flattened, but not flat, bottom. A sharply ridged deck not only expanded the interior, it also helped to shed waves. The beam of approximately 30 inches gave the kayak excellent stability and, combined with a sealable waterproof gut-skin parka and one or two recovery techniques, made it very seaworthy. The wide cockpit facilitated storage of game and also allowed two people to ride back to back with ease. Margaret Lantis recorded a story in which the passenger acted as a bow-and-arrow-equipped "tail-gunner" during a war raid (1946:306).

The 30 inch beam of the kayak in Figure 50 makes this kayak the widest in the Arctic while the average length of just over fifteen feet makes it almost the shortest of Eskimo kayaks. A Hooper Bay informant said that this length kayak handled better in heavy seas than a longer vessel.

Paddling Techniques

Because the kayaks of this area were so broad and deep, use of the double-bladed paddle was difficult. Consequently it was used only for speed, often from a kneeling position. Kneeling and occasionally standing were paddling positions used with the single-bladed paddle as well. A short paddle was used to scull the kayak to within harpooning distance of sea mammals. It could be noiselessly operated with one hand on the side away from a dozing animal with a weapon held at the ready in the other hand.

Figure 52. Nunivak Island kayak frame photographed by Edward S. Curtis (The North American Indian, facing p. 44) in 1929. The bow and stern represent the head and tail of the owner's helping spirit. Photograph courtesy of the National Museums of Canada, Ottawa.

Photograph by Mark Daughhetee

Kayak Accessories

A small sled was an important kayak accessory and was used to haul the kayak to the floe edge and over ice floes. When not in use, it was stowed on the afterdeck. The foredeck carried extra paddles, gaffs, and a great variety of specialized spears, darts and harpoons for use against different seals and waterfowl.

The hunter wore a gutskin parka cut full to allow the parka to be sealed with a tie around the cockpit coaming. Sealskin formed the underarm part of the parka to prevent chafe due to constant rubbing on the cockpit coaming while paddling. The parka was sealed tightly around the face with a drawstring, and fishskin mitts with sealskin palms had their long cuffs tied tightly over the parka sleeves. Thus equipped, a paddler could capsize and remain dry except for his face. The ability to right oneself after a capsize was reported for this area. Hooper Bay informants however, could not remember this as being possible or important.

Bearded seal stomachs with a fine mesh grass covering were carried inside as a type of canteen.

In rough seas these could be emptied, inflated with air, and shoved in the kayak ends to act as extra buoyancy chambers should the kayak fill with water. Also inside the kayak was a wooden slat seat on top of a woven grass mat. Both helped to keep dirt from working down between stringers and cover where it could chafe through.. Another grass mat was carried inside to use as a windbreak when butchering game on an ice floe. It could also be used as a sail when two kayaks were tied together. A kayak sled was put crosswise over the foredecks and the mat secured to it in front.

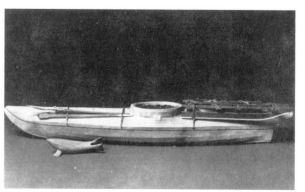

Photograph by Mark Daughhetee

Figure 53. Wooden kayak frame from Nunivak Island. Length 188.5". Collection Alaska State Museum. II-A-5024.

Figure 54. Kayak model from Nunivak Island. Skin covered wooden framework with ivory keel plates. Accessories include wooden sled with ivory runners, wood seal float, ivory tipped bird spear, blubber hook, snowshoes and paddles. Length 25". Collection Sheldon Jackson Museum. II.0.23.

Photograph by David Zimmerly

Kayak Use

Other than its use for sea mammal hunting, the kayak was used when spearing waterfowl, fishing, racing, gathering firewood, occasional clamming by the women, transporting goods and ferrying people across bays, streams and rivers. One informant saw six people in a kayak crossing a stream—two in the cockpit sitting back to back, one prone in the forward hull, one prone in the after hull and one each prone on forward and after decks.

In her 1940 trip to Hooper Bay, Lantis reported 63 kayaks in a population of 360 people (1946:164). By 1978, with over twice that population, the number of useable kayaks had dwindled to less than a dozen and all of these appeared to have been made ten to twenty years earlier.

Hooper Bay is the last kayak-using community of any size in this area of Alaska. It provided a recent, last live examination of kayak building techniques.

Photograph by David Zimmerly

Figure 55. Cockpit of Silas Tomaganak's modern Hooper Bay canvas-covered kayak. Note salt-grass mat, iron hook for towing seals and sled on aft deck. Fig. 55 and 56 courtesy of the National Museums of Canada, Ottawa.

Figure 56. Silas Tomaganak with spotted seal just towed in by kayak. Note kayak sled on aft deck.

Hooper Bay Kayak Technology

This community shows archaeological evidence of over 600 years of continuous occupation. It is similar in many respects to the communities studied by Curtis and Lantis on nearby Nunivak Island. Hooper Bay had a different dialect and slightly less complex ritual life than Nunivak Island, but the kayak complex as a whole was generally similar for all coastal Yukon-Kuskokwim Delta Eskimo.

When I first arrived in Hooper Bay in 1976 [more detail on Hooper Bay kayak construction may be found in Zimmerly 1978 and 1979], I was fortunate to find sixty-nine year old Dick Bunyan, who was a skilled kayak-maker with over twenty kayaks and two umiaks (open skin boats) to his credit. He agreed to construct a kayak frame for the National Museums of Canada from driftwood using intermediate technology consisting of a few modern hand tools plus steel-bladed traditional items such as an adze and curved carving knife.

Dick selected a large stump from a pile of driftwood he had gathered and, using an axe and wooden wedges, split it into pieces that would be suitable for the curved deck beams of the kayak. He explained through an interpreter that maximum

Photograph by David Zimmerly

strength was obtained by having wood with a grain that was already curved the way the finished piece would be.

Dick's adze was made from an old hatchet blade, and with it he could shape a piece of wood to look as though it had been smoothed with a plane. No sandpaper was ever used. The curved carving knife, made from a muskrat trap spring, was the perfect tool to hollow out all concave surfaces.

Dick's only measuring device was a 75 cm-long stick that was used to transfer measurements first determined anthropometrically. For example, the diameter of the hole in the bow is equal to the width of the closed fist with the thumb outstretched. The diameter of the cockpit coaming is equal to the distance from the armpit to the first joints of the fingers that grip the coaming. All parts of the kayak were similarly measured. Each community had its own standard set of anthropometric measurements which accounted for great intra-community uniformity as most of the men were of the same general build.

Figure 58. Upper and lower bow pieces, faired and tied together. The ends of the stringers fit snugly against the concave portion of the lower bow block to prevent chafe against the cover. Fig. 58-62 courtesy of the National Museums of Canada, Ottawa.

Figure 57. Kayaks on the beach at Hooper Bay, Alaska. Photo by Edward S. Curtis, 1927. Collection Alaska State Museum. V-C-86.

After the final shaping of the deck beams, Dick carved out the upper bow block and the stern handhold. He then attached them to their associated deck stringers with notched scarf joints. The deck stringers were made from pieces split out of a large driftwood log. The splitting was done using small hardwood wedges carved from a broken hickory axe handle.

The gunwales were fashioned from one driftwood log that Dick first squared up with a hatchet and adze and then halved by sawing with a portable circular saw. The saw-cut sides became the outer sides of the gunwales in the finished product.

The general method of work was to first split out pieces from the driftwood log or stump, then rough-shape with a hatchet, and final-shape with the adze and curved carving knife. In this fashion Dick prefabricated all 57 pieces of the kayak.

Photograph by David Zimmerly

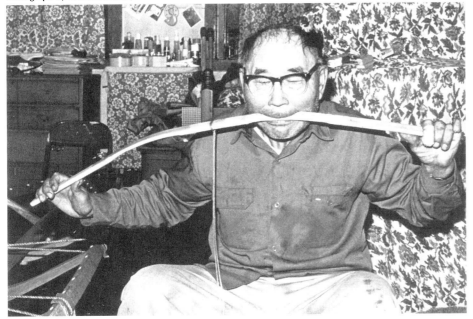

Figure 59. Dick Bunyan bending a kayak rib without steaming it. His teeth act as a clamp to prevent the outer fibers from splitting while crushing the inboard ones to facilitate bending.

In a little over three weeks the parts were complete and ready for pre-assembly trimming, painting and bending. The gunwales were joined at the ends and spread apart in the middle to check for even bending. One gunwale, judged less springy than the other, was planed down a bit on the outboard side, rechecked and pronounced finished. The ribs were bent cold by clamping the teeth down on them and bending by hand, tying the ends together with a nylon cord that was later used as the rib/stringer tie.

At this point Dick enlisted the aid of several neighbors. Aloysius Hale formed the outer coaming lip into a circle by spot heating it with hot water, bending it with his hands and tightening up a line connecting the ends. I painted the gunwales, ribs and stringers while another neighbor cut mortises into the gunwales for the deck beams and ribs. Dick supervised closely.

The paint that I used was a powdered red ocher colored rock traded from Nelson Island. The powder was mixed with a little water and rubbed on the wood with a cloth. I could discover no functional reason for the use of this paint. Dick told me, *"We've always done it this way."*

When all was ready the deck beams were fitted into the gunwales. The gunwale ends were then bolted together, and the bow and stern pieces added along with the deck stringers. While this was all very straightforward, the next step in the assembly was rather critical.

Bering Sea kayaks have a slight reverse sheer achieved in the following manner. The gunwale/deck beam/deck stringer assembly was placed upside down supported by two boxes. The keelson pieces, attached to their respective lower bow and stern blocks, were next fitted into place. As they were prefabricated extra long, they overlapped amidships. By trimming them slightly short and joining them with a notched scarf joint, the ends of the kayak were put in tension, resulting in the gunwales bending upwards (remember the frame is upside down), causing reverse sheer to form.

The keelson was then blocked and temporarily tied to prevent any rocker from forming. The first rib was fitted in amidships and the others worked in toward each end.

Next the stringers were fitted to length and held in place with more temporary ties. A length of twine was used for the rib/stringer tie which runs athwartships from gunwale to gunwale. Following other trimming and special lashings, the framework was turned rightside up. The cockpit coaming was lashed temporarily in place while the gunwale-to-coaming stanchions were fitted.

With the addition of some touchup paint and trimming, the kayak frame was finished, exactly one month from when it was started.

Present Use

Presently, other than limited use for seal hunting and fishing, the kayak has ceased to function in any viable fashion. Many of the taboos and ceremonies surrounding the kayak complex were eliminated after the introduction of Christianity. Most kayak functions were supplanted by the motorized skiff. With the decline of the men's house, the ready sources of knowledge and help for kayak building became problematic. The final reason for the decline of the kayak is that kayak construction is very labor intensive. Few people are willing or able to devote that much time when they can purchase or build a substitute or get along without.

Figure 60. Dick Bunyan watching Aloysius Hale fit the crucial first rib in the kayak.

Photograph by David Zimmerly

Figure 61. The cockpit coaming is temporarily tied to the frame in order to fit the cockpit coaming to gunwale stanchions.

Photograph by David Zimmerly

Norton Sound

The Norton Sound kayak type was found from St. Michael in southern Norton Sound up to the north side of the sound where the Bering Strait kayak type predominates. This kayak shares many construction and cross section similarities (see Figure 65) with the Nunivak and Hooper Bay kayaks. However, it is narrower and is visually distinguished from the others by the straight line of the deck ridge in profile as seen in Figure 64. The characteristic handgrips on the ends are formed by extensions of the fore and aft deck stringers.

The most detailed description of the Norton Sound kayak is found in a report submitted to the U.S. Coast and Geodetic Survey in 1899 by Dr. H. M. W. Edmonds. His work was eclipsed by E. W. Nelson's comprehensive work, *The Eskimo About Bering Strait*, published that same year. Edmonds' report was not published until 1966 when the University of Alaska Press released a version edited by Dorothy Jean Ray.

Figure 63. An unusual kayak model showing three hatches and a Bering Sea bow configuration. Collected by G.T. Emmons in Nome in the late 1800s. There are no known examples of full-size three-hole Bering Sea kayaks. Length 40.5". Collection Alaska State Museum. II-A-2558.

Photograph by David Zimmerly

Figure 62. Author David Zimmerly and Aloysius Hale relax after lunch while seal hunting from the floe edge.

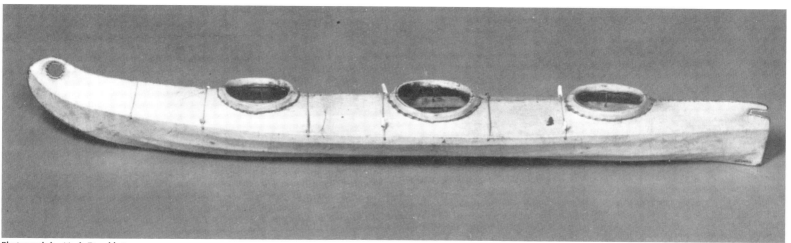

Photograph by Mark Daughhetee

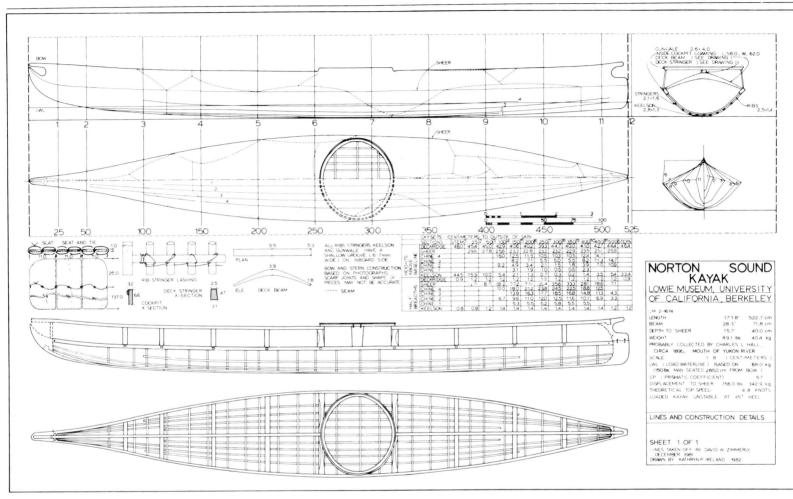

NORTON SOUND KAYAK
LOWIE MUSEUM, UNIVERSITY OF CALIFORNIA, BERKELEY

LM 2-1674

LENGTH	17'1.8"	522.7 cm
BEAM	28.3"	71.8 cm
DEPTH TO SHEER	15.7"	40.0 cm
WEIGHT	89.1 lbs	40.4 kg

PROBABLY COLLECTED BY CHARLES L. HALL, CIRCA 1895, MOUTH OF YUKON RIVER
SCALE 1:8 (CENTIMETERS)
LWL (LOAD WATERLINE) BASED ON 68.0 kg (150 lbs MAN SEATED 286.0 cm FROM BOW)
CP (PRISMATIC COEFFICIENT) .57
DISPLACEMENT TO SHEER 756.0 lbs 342.9 kg
THEORETICAL TOP SPEED 4.8 KNOTS
LOADED KAYAK UNSTABLE AT 45° HEEL

LINES AND CONSTRUCTION DETAILS

SHEET 1 OF 1

LINES TAKEN OFF BY DAVID W. ZIMMERLY, DECEMBER 1981
DRAWN BY KATHRYN P. IRELAND, 1982

ALL RIBS, STRINGERS, KEELSON AND GUNWALE HAVE A SHALLOW GROOVE (6-7mm WIDE) ON INBOARD SIDE

BOW AND STERN CONSTRUCTION BASED ON PHOTOGRAPHS. SCARF JOINTS AND SHAPE OF PIECES MAY NOT BE ACCURATE

----- SEAM

His description of the Norton Sound kayak is centered around those built and used in St. Michael (Ray 1966). I consider the St. Michael style kayak to be the archetype for the Norton Sound type.

In the variety of kayak most commonly seen at St. Michael and over this whole region, the lines of the boat are fine, the general effect is that of swiftness, with moderate stability and carrying power. The sheer line is straight, except where broken by the coaming of the cockpit, which projects from one to two

Figure 64. Construction details of a Norton Sound kayak, c. 1895. Length 17' 1.8". University of California, Lowie Museum. Sheet (1 of 1). Line drawing IV-E-23M © Canadian Museum of Civilization.

Figure 65. View towards bow of kayak in fig. 64. Collection Lowie Museum of Anthropology, University of California at Berkeley. LM 2-1674.

Figure 66. Kayak storage racks and fish drying racks in Unalakleet on Norton Sound. Photograph taken by Ray B. Dame, July 1938. Photograph courtesy of the Anchorage Museum of History and Art.

inches above the body of the boat. The prow has a narrow opening and is shaped as shown. The stern line is vertical and cut into at the upper part by the grip...(Ray 1966:56).

The Norton Sound kayak was, like most other Eskimo kayaks, mainly a hunting tool used for going after seals, sea otters, waterfowl and fish. However, both Edmonds and Nelson commented on the remarkable carrying capacity of this kayak. Edmonds stated that:

Two persons often go out in the same kayak, both sitting up in the one cockpit, back to back. The front man, of course, does the paddling. In case of great emergency, as many as four have been known to be carried in a single one-holed kayak. Two of them lie

down, stowed well fore and aft, while two sit up back to back in the cockpit....

Considerable freight can be carried in a kayak, such as flour, fish, seal oil, &c. These are stored fore and aft in the interior. Even on top considerable weight and bulk may be carried in safety, as, for instance, a light sled or a pile of wood, even when it is so rough that the waves break over the prow (Ray 1966:57-58).

Figure 66 shows a Norton Sound kayak stored upside down (museums take notice) on lashed crossed poles that conform to the same angle as the ridged deck. Drying fish are also visible on nearby racks.

E. W. Nelson described another way that Norton Sound kayakers hauled freight and combined it with sailing.

In journeying on rivers or along the coast, the Eskimo frequently fasten two kaiaks side by side by lashing cross-sticks against the front and rear of the manholes with rawhide cord. A kind of platform of sticks is also made across the deck, on which small loads of goods are placed. These are fixed usually behind the manhole, although at times a load is carried both before and behind the occupant.

On one occasion, near St. Michael, I saw two kaiaks lashed together in this way, with a man in each, and just behind them was placed a small pile of household goods, consisting mainly of bedding, upon which sat a woman. In front a small mast, held in position by guys, had been raised on a crosspiece lashed on the decks near the front crosscords, and a small sail, made from parchment-like gut skin, was raised. This odd-looking vessel was making very good time on a small stream before the wind (Nelson 1899:221).

Figure 67 shows a Norton Sound kayaker throwing a harpoon using a throwing board (atlatl). On the forward deck is his coiled-up harpoon line and wooden tray to hold it. Visible on the aft deck is an inflated skin float which is attached to the other end of the harpoon line. The kayaker's highly decorated wooden visor-hat shields him from the sun and salt spray. It was also a high-value trade item. A similar hat among the Aleut was worth a one-hole kayak in trade.

Most early explorers and writers do not tell us much about Eskimo paddling techniques. Edmonds is an exception.

The paddle used is from three to four and a half feet long, and has a medium sized blade about four or five inches wide, flat on one side and with a single medium ridge and two side grooves on the other. The handle ends in a cross stick about three inches long, against which the upper hand strikes every time the paddle is changed over from one side to the other. These Eskimo always shift the paddle from side to side, never paddling continuously on one side unless it be in crossing a rapid stream to keep the canoe headed in the right direction. In quiet waters, two strokes are usually taken on one side and then two on the other side, the canoe twisting slightly from one side to the other of the course. Winds or waves or tide may compel more strokes on one side than on the other. Turning is accomplished by giving a wide sweep outwards with the paddle or by backing

Figure 67. Photo of a Norton Sound kayaker throwing a harpoon with an atlatl. Photograph by E. W. Nelson taken between 1877 and 1881. Photograph courtesy of the Smithsonian Institution National Anthropological Archives.

Figure 68. Model Norton Sound style kayak collected by G. T. Emmons in the late 1800s. Length 23.5". Collection Alaska State Museum. II-A-2690.

Figure 69. Unknown Eskimo artist in 1890s pictures three different versions of Norton Sound kayaks. Note spears and darts on the starboard side decks held in place by deck lines. Photograph courtesy of the Smithsonian Institution National Anthropological Archives.

water or tailing the paddle but not by the skillful twist of the paddle as practiced by S. E. Alaskan Indians.

By holding the paddle in one hand with the handle resting against the outside of the arm to above the elbow, the [kayak], in close quarters, may be quickly maneuvered with much dexterity. With paddle-blade resting on the water and the handle held firmly at the front edge of the cockpit, it serves as an outrigger and keeps the canoe steady while lying to for any purpose in a rough sea. In such cases, neither the double nor the single paddle is passed through the loops of seal thong on the kayak.

Besides the single paddle, the double paddle is also used but not so commonly, and nearly always a single paddle is also carried along in the same kayak. The double bladed paddle is very long and slender, with blades that look ridiculously small. It is used for rapid work on long stretches and is put aside immediately on approaching shallow water or the destination, and the single paddle used to complete the trip. In case the paddles are lost, any light stick or spear will serve to get home with....

There are fewer differences in paddles than in the kayaks (Ray 1966:59).

There are a number of Norton Sound kayak models that have two and three hatches. Edmonds said that:

These, however, are not characteristic of the country. They are modeled after those found in the Aleutian Islands and usually made to order by some traveler or trader and passed over into the hands of the Eskimo (Ray 1966:60).

By the end of the nineteenth century, the King Island type of kayak with a more upswept bow was being introduced more and more into the Norton Sound area. The result, implied Edmonds (p. 56) was a better sea boat than the St. Michael type.

Figure 69 shows three slightly different versions of Norton Sound kayaks. The bottom kayak shows the King Island influence of an upturned bow with the handhold in a loop raised above the deck.

Photograph by Ken DeRoux

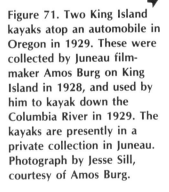

Figure 70. Eskimo hunting hat from Norton Sound area, made of wood and decorated with ivory carvings, grass and feathers. Collected by Sheldon Jackson in the late 1800s. Collection Sheldon Jackson Museum. II.F.13.

Figure 71. Two King Island kayaks atop an automobile in Oregon in 1929. These were collected by Juneau filmmaker Amos Burg on King Island in 1928, and used by him to kayak down the Columbia River in 1929. The kayaks are presently in a private collection in Juneau. Photograph by Jesse Sill, courtesy of Amos Burg.

Figure 72. Lines and construction section of a King Island kayak from the collection of R.T. Wallen in Juneau, shown in Fig. 71. This specimen, which consists of the framework only, weighs 37 pounds. It is the classic King Island Bering Strait type. Length 14' 10.1", width 25.3".

BERING STRAIT

In 1929 the famous photographer/ethnographer Edward S. Curtis was told the story of the origin of King Island.

A man, who lived on the mainland, while fishing in a river near the Sawtooth mountains, once speared a large bullhead from his kaiak. By lashing its tail violently, the struggling fish so widened the river that it formed Salt lake. The fish towed the kaiak swiftly down the stream, but at the mouth the man was able to heave in on the line until near enough to cast a second spear. The pain-maddened fish flung about so furiously that it formed what is now called Grantley Harbor.

The bullhead towed the kaiak out of sight of land before the man was able to make his kill. Then he towed the monster by passing a line through its mouth. He paddled long and hard. Tired out, he looked about and saw that he had not moved even the length of a kaiak. Glancing over his shoulder, he was astounded to see that the fish had turned into an island (King island); the hole where the line was attached can still be seen (1930:105).

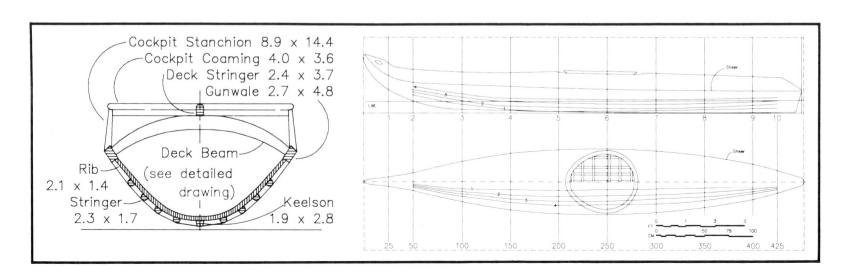

Cockpit Stanchion 8.9 x 14.4
Cockpit Coaming 4.0 x 3.6
Deck Stringer 2.4 x 3.7
Gunwale 2.7 x 4.8

Deck Beam
(see detailed drawing)

Rib
2.1 x 1.4

Stringer
2.3 x 1.7

Keelson
1.9 x 2.8

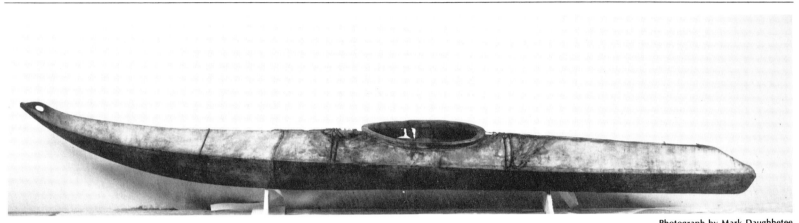

Photograph by Mark Daughhetee

The King Island kayak is the epitome of the Bering Strait kayak type. The variations on this style were found all along the Seward Peninsula coast from somewhere east of Cape Nome in the south to somewhere east of Cape Espenberg in Kotzebue Sound. Major historic settlements in this area include Nome, King Island, Teller, Brevig Mission, Wales and Shishmaref.

The builders of the Bering Strait kayaks belong to the Inupiat speaking Eskimos which include all those in North Alaska, Canada and Greenland. From Norton Sound south the Eskimos are Yupik speaking (the two linguistic groups are mutually unintelligible). Yet the Bering Strait kayak is more like the kayaks to the south than those to the north.

Kayak Construction

Like the Nunivak and Hooper Bay kayaks, the Bering Strait kayak, which averages 14 feet 9 inches long by 24.6 inches wide, is strongly built, multi-chined, with a ridged deck and cockpit large enough for two people sitting back to back. Elements of internal construction techniques were

also more closely allied to the southern Bering Sea kayak styles than to the North Alaska ones. But the Bering Strait kayak is shorter and narrower than the kayaks to the south. The average weight of a Bering Strait kayak is also reduced, being just under 40 pounds compared to near 60 pounds for the Bering Sea kayaks.

We can see how light these kayaks are from the ease with which the hunter in Figure 74 carries his craft.

Figure 73. King Island kayak from the late 19th century. Length 14'8". Collection Sheldon Jackson Museum. II-E-95.

Figure 74. King Island-type kayak. Photograph by the Lomen Brothers, courtesy of the Glenbow Museum, Calgary, Alberta.

The King Island kayak frame in Figure 75 shows the closely spaced ribs and naturally-curved deck beams which account for much of the strength of this kayak.

All Bering Strait kayaks have bows that are swept upwards to some degree. Some bows come to a point, such as at Cape Espenberg. Others have integral hand holes for carrying while others have a skin carrying loop. Stern configurations also exhibit some differences with carrying handholds varying from skin loops to extensions of the aft deck stringer to a cut away stern that slopes from the deck stringer down to the gunwales with no handhold.

The kayak was covered with bearded seal, and sometimes on King Island, with bearded seal at the bow and split walrus in the stern (Heath 1972:8). Most of the kayak framework was made from spruce, with naturally-curved spruce roots used for the curved deck beams. Ribs were of birch, probably one of the major trade items from the Kotzebue Sound area. Willow was often used for the cockpit coaming.

Figure 75. King Island kayak frame viewed from the stern. Note the kayak sled parts lying bundled on the ground at the top right of the photo. Photograph by Dorothy Jean Ray taken in King Island Village, Nome, 1950.

Cape Espenberg

The Cape Espenberg subtype of Bering Strait kayak is distinguished by the absence of a built-in bow handhold causing the bow profile to come to a sharper point.

This type is well-illustrated in Figure 76.

Minus the thong handhold on the stern, the kayak in Figure 77 looks much like the Cape Espenberg type, but it is from Teller, Alaska, a coastal settlement east of Nome.

Photograph by Mark Daughhetee

King Island

The King Island kayak is the best made and strongest of the Bering Strait kayaks. Henry Elliott, writing in 1886, tells us why.

> Long experience at plunging through surf with their handsomely made kayaks, and returning to land on these perilous shores of King's Island, has made the Ookivok people the boldest and the best watermen in the north. Their little skin canoes are of the finest construction, and their surplus time is largely passed in carving walrus-ivory into all fashions of rude design for barter in the summer...(Elliott 1886:427).

E. W. Nelson, writing a little later than Elliott, mentioned the long-distance traveling done by the King Island kayakers.

> These kaiaks are strongly made; they are used in the stormy waters of the strait, and sometimes are taken even to the Siberian coast of the strait and to St. Lawrence island (Nelson 1899:220).

Figure 76. Cape Espenberg type kayak. Note the sharp bow configuration compared to Fig. 72. Length 14' 7.5". Collection Sheldon Jackson Museum. II.Y.34.

Figure 77. Bering Strait kayak in Grantley Harbor, Teller, Alaska. Photograph courtesy of the University of Alaska Archives, Lomen Family Collection.

56

Figure 78. Rack for harpoon line, also called a "float board." Note the four ivory seals with inset eyes of beads and wood. King Island. Hoop 18" x 16", legs 36". Collection Alaska State Museum. II-A-4205.

Figure 79. Drag handle and plugs for seal hunting. Wood, ivory, and skin. King Island. Length of drag, 11.75". Collection Alaska State Museum. II-A-359.

Figure 80. Throwing stick used for added leverage when throwing a dart or a spear. Wood, ivory, glass beads and copper. King Island. Length 16.5". Collection Alaska State Museum. II-A-4171.

Figure 81. Sled used for transporting a kayak over ice floes. Wood, with bone runners. Length 58.5". Collection Sheldon Jackson Museum. II.X.683.

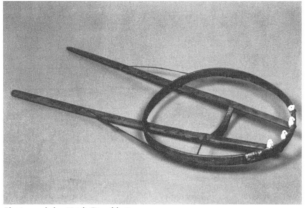
Photograph by Mark Daughhetee

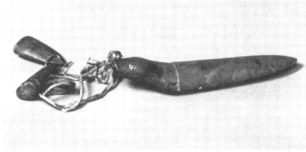
Photograph by Mark Daughhetee

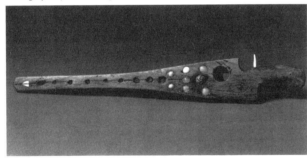
Photograph by Mark Daughhetee

Photograph by Mark Daughhetee

Kayak Accessories

While the single-bladed paddle (anguun), about one armspan long, was preferred for most uses, the double-bladed paddle (pautik), about one and one-half arms spans long, was used when additional speed was desired (Heath 1972:24-25).

For added stability when paddling without a load, a large 25-pound rock was placed behind the paddler as ballast (Heath 1972:27).

For sea mammal hunting the following equipment was carried:

On the foredeck
boathook (nivsuun)
gaff—shoulder to opposite arm fingertips length (itun)
spare single-bladed paddle (anguun)
harpoon (kan—shaft only?)
harpoon line-tray (asaluuk)
coiled harpoon line (aliq)
bird dart (nugit)
throwing board (nuqsaq)

On the afterdeck
inflated sealskin float (avataq)
small kayak sled

Inside
rifle
bearded sealskin seat (irngmalin)
miscellaneous items

Worn by kayaker
kayaking jacket—gutskin with sleeves made from walrus heart skin covering (imarnitik)
gutskin raincoat (kavitaq)

Kayak Use

The King Island kayak was used from April until December when the sea froze over until the following spring. Walrus were hunted from April to June. Miscellaneous hunting and fishing was done from kayaks during the summer followed by important bearded seal hunting in the fall.

Launching Procedure

The King Island kayakers are famous for their unique launching methods. Captain Hooper described how it was done in 1880.

The natives of this Arctic Gibraltar are very expert with the "kyack." It is said that when the surf is breaking against the perpendicular sides of the island, should it be necessary to launch a canoe for any purpose, the native who is to embark takes his seat in his "kyack" as near the surf as he can approach with safety, secures his water-proof shirt, made of the intestines of the walrus, to the

rim of the hatch, grasps his paddle, and, watching a favorable opportunity, gives a signal to two men who stand in readiness, and is thrown entirely clear of the surf. These "kyacks" are probably the finest in the world, but, owing to the rough service they have to perform, are made somewhat heavier than those in use in Kotzebue sound... (Hooper 1881:15).

A less spectacular launch method from a mainland beach involved facing the kayak into the sea while on the beach and then waiting for a wave to come in at which time the kayaker used a single-bladed paddle on each side to simultaneously take his weight off the kayak and drive it forward into the surf. This technique is shown in Figure 82.

Figure 82. Preparing to launch a kayak into the surf from a beach. Photograph by the Fifth Thule Expedition, courtesy of the Danish National Museum, Copenhagen.

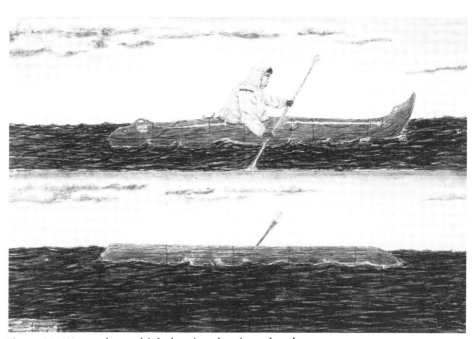

Figure 83. Watercolor and ink drawing showing a kayak roll by Kivetoruk Moses(1900-1982) of Nome, Alaska. Collection Alaska State Museum. V-A-709.

Figure 84. Preparing to roll the kayak. The man on the left has just finished sealing himself into his kayak with his gutskin parka. The man on the right will act as his second. Fig. 84-87 by the Lomen Brothers, courtesy of the Glenbow Museum, Calgary, Alberta.

Figure 85. The paddler has just capsized the kayak to the preferred starboard side.

Figure 86. The paddler is now completely upside down, but starting the capsize recovery techniques underwater.

Capsize Recovery

In case of a capsize, recovery techniques (kitunarautaq) were developed using the single-bladed paddle. The kayaker always tried to capsize to starboard while holding the paddle with the blade to port. This method of holding the paddle prevented it from being knocked out of the paddler's hand during the roll (Heath 1972:30).

According to John Heath, a kayaker had alternatives for surviving a capsize other than righting the kayak.

> ...he might still survive a capsize by crawling up inside his kayak and awaiting rescue by his comrades. There was enough air trapped inside a capsized kayak to provide several minutes of breathing. The kayak jacket had a topknot-like projection at the rear of the hood. If a man was wearing his jacket when he capsized, he could grab this projection and pull it forward so that his face went up inside the hood to find an airspace for breathing (1972:31).

Figures 84-90 provide us with a unique set of illustrations of the King Island capsize recovery techniques. The series includes photos taken by the Lomen Brothers of Nome plus several shot by the Danish Fifth Thule Expedition. The man doing the rolling is the same in both sets of pictures. He was probably a professional at it since very few men still knew how to roll a kayak in this century.

Hunting

Spring hunting involved logistical problems with getting the kayak to open water, across ice-floes, back to open water and so forth. This was accomplished with a small kayak sled that was carried on the aft deck. Figure 91 shows two Bering Strait seal hunters with their kayak sleds.

It is no accident that several hunters are shown together in Figure 90 above:

> When men hunt in kaiaks, two of the craft go out together, and if successful they tow the carcass between them (Curtis 1930:101).

After rifles were introduced, the sea mammal hunting technique changed from that of pre-European methods.

> When a seal or a walrus was sighted, the kayaker stalked it to within firing range, then shot it and paddled rapidly to within about twenty feet before throwing his harpoon. As soon as the harpoon hit, the hunter threw his

Figure 91. Bering Strait hunters searching for game. Lomen Brothers photograph, courtesy of the Glenbow Museum, Calgary, Alberta.

float overboard. He then followed the float if the animal was only wounded and as soon as it tired enough to approach, he dispatched it. Wooden wound plugs were inserted in the dead animal where required and when necessary, an implement was inserted under the skin and worked around to make an air space, then the area was inflated orally and plugged to provide flotation.

Small seals were brought home inside the kayak, but large seals or walrus were either butchered on the ice floes so that meat could be stowed below decks or towed home. Two kayaks were used to tow a walrus (Heath 1972:28-29).

Freighting

Trading in the summer was a major activity attended to by Bering Strait Eskimos. They traveled to the trading sites by both kayak and umiak. Trade fairs

at Cape Blossom in Kotzebue Sound drew people from Point Hope to Nome including the Diomedes. In 1880 Captain Hooper arrived at Cape Blossom in July.

These natives collect for the purpose of trading not only with vessels, but also with each other. The coast natives bring oil, walrus-hides, and seal-skins; those from Cape Prince of Wales bring whiskey, arms, tobacco and skins of tame reindeer, which they purchase from the Tchuktchis. These articles are exchanged with the natives of the interior for furs — wolf, fox, marten, mink, &c (Hooper 1881:26).

Much trade also took place at King Island when whalers or other large ships stopped. A favorite method for hauling goods was to lash two kayaks together forming a catamaran (*kilukmiik*).

The two craft were pushed together so that they touched at the gunwale and the cockpit rim; in this position, they were each heeled inward slightly, which helped keep them from taking seas. The short sticks which were

Figure 92. Kayakers come out from King Island to trade with itinerant ships. Note the pairs lashed together to form a catamaran. Photograph by the Lomen Brothers, courtesy of the Glenbow Museum, Calgary, Alberta.

carried on the afterdeck for attaching the float served to bridge the space between the kayaks. One pair of these were laid across the deck ridges at the pair of deck straps forward of the cockpit and one pair was mounted in the same manner aft the cockpit. About four turns of lashing ran from the middle of each pair of these straight down to the gunwales and around the deck straps. This held the kayaks together. A sealskin float was sometimes stuck in between the foredecks of the two kayaks to keep out splash. When paddling the catamaran, the kayakers often sat on the after edge of the cockpit (Heath 1972:29-30).

E. W. Nelson also mentioned the use of kayak catamarans for freighting.

When the CORWIN reached King island, in Bering strait, one stormy day in the summer of 1881, the islanders lashed their kaiaks in pairs, and came off with piles of furs and other articles of trade heaped up on the decks behind the manholes (1899:221).

Two-hole Bering Strait Kayaks

The idea for two-hole kayaks such as built by the Aleut and Pacific Eskimo spread to Norton Sound and Bering Strait. The type was often made on contract for white explorers or traders and then came into the hands of the Eskimos when the latter no longer needed them. The type was not often seen, but at least three specimens have ended up in American museums.

Figure 93. Two-hole Bering Strait kayak. Photograph courtesy of the Anchorage Museum of History and Art.

North Alaska, in terms of kayak types, includes the area from Kotzebue Sound east to the Canadian border. The general kayak in use was the inland type with several variations. In general there is a Kotzebue Sound/Point Barrow type, an inland Nunamiut Eskimo type and a shortened version I call the North Alaska Retrieval type.

Kayak Construction

This kayak type follows the general construction practices of all Eskimo kayaks. The kayak is generally long and very narrow with a rounded cross section and a rockered bottom—the ideal form for speed, but very tippy. There is some reverse sheer near the cockpit area, but the ends often curve up. The decks are flat except in front of the cockpit coaming where the deck rises sharply to meet the highly raked coaming. This serves to shed waves and keep the kayaker dry in the absence of a spray skirt.

The hull shape is multi-chined with the bottom of the hull cross section fairly flat. The ribs are closely spaced and there are three longitudinal stringers on each side plus the keelson. The stringers are fastened to the ribs with continuous ties that run the

Figure 94. "Noatak Kaiaks," by Edward Curtis, 1927, showing typical North Alaskan kayak styles. Collection Alaska State Museum. V-C-67.

length of the stringers. This contrasts with kayaks south of Bering Strait all of which have rib/stringer ties that run transversely across each rib from port to starboard.

While the coastal Eskimos from Kotzebue to Barrow covered their kayaks with sealskin, more inland dwelling Eskimos along the Noatak River covered a similar kayak type with caribou skin. They used the craft for muskrat hunting on the reedy lagoons and for spearing caribou as they crossed rivers and lakes.

We will look at the three subtypes and see how they differed from the basic construction and how they were used.

Kotzebue Sound/Point Barrow

The type is just over 17 feet long and about 18.5 inches in beam. Except for a bit of reverse sheer in the cockpit area, the deck is fairly flat in profile. Figure 95 shows this kayak type. The specimen weighs just under 30 pounds.

Figure 95. Lines and construction details of a pre-1898 North Alaska Kotzebue Sound/Point Barrow-type kayak. Length 17′ 2.9″. University of California, Lowie Museum. Sheet (1 of 1). Line drawing IV-E-20M © Canadian Museum of Civilization.

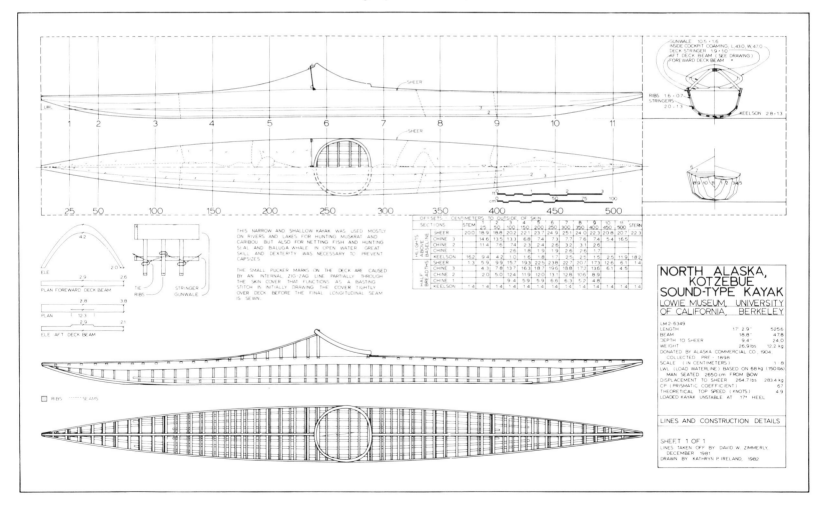

Photograph by Mark Daughhetee

Figure 96. Typical North Alaska Kotzebue/Point Barrow style kayak collected by Sheldon Jackson in 1890. Length 17'7.5". Collection Sheldon Jackson Museum. II.Y.33.

Figure 97. An Eskimo traveling over the sea ice with kayak on sled while seal hunting. Canadian Arctic Expedition 1913-1916 photo by George H. Wilkins courtesy of National Museum of Canada, Ottawa.

Captain Hooper described this type.

The "kyack" used by the natives on Kotzebue sound, and, in fact, along the entire coast to Point Barrow, is a marvel of speed and beauty. It is very narrow and light, and great skill is required in its management (Hooper 1881:25).

Figure 96 shows a typical North Alaska kayak specimen from the Sheldon Jackson Museum in Sitka.

Kayak Use

Kotzebue Sound-type kayaks were not used for open water hunting when the sea was rough, but were used for seal hunting from the edge of the ice in early winter and spring. The kayak sled was used to haul the kayak over the ice to open water. Figure 97 shows the kayak being man-hauled on a sled.

Hunting the Beluga Whale

Beluga whale hunting was a community affair with many kayaks and umiaks involved. The week before the hunt was filled with feasting, games and dancing which, it was believed, would bring a fair on-shore wind driving the belugas close to shore. Amulets for good luck in the hunt were often hung inside the kayak. Dorothy Jean Ray relates, *"Nelson unsuccessfully tried to buy a wooden beluga-like image hanging from the framework of a kayak at Kotzebue Sound in 1881, [but] its owner said that he would die if he parted with it"* (1981:23).

Edward S. Curtis described what happened when the whales were sighted.

Then the boats and kaiaks put out, each hunter armed with two spears and two flint knives. They form a long line to seaward of the belugas and drive them in-shore. The older hunters, in kaiaks, cast the first spears and drive the animals into shallow water, where they become stranded and helpless.

The men stab them in the blow-holes until they are dead. Kaiaks are used in the surrounding and killing, because they are much more mobile than the larger skin boats. The crews of these, too, hunt and kill, but their chief usefulness is in towing the catch to the village (Curtis 1930 Vol.20:163).

Captain Hooper also described a beluga whale hunt that he observed in 1880.

The "beluga" are hunted in kyacks; a dozen or more natives take up a position near the entrance of some bay, where they can see them as they come in with the tide. As soon as they have passed, the natives paddle out behind them, and, by shouting and beating the water, drive them into shoal water, where they are easily dispatched with flint spears. According to their tradition, to kill the beluga with any other weapon, would entail endless misfortune upon the guilty party (Hooper 1881:59).

Photograph by Mark Daughhetee

an elliptical cross section, *"...with the greatest width at right angles to the plane of the blades so to present the greatest resistance to the strain of paddling"* (Murdoch 1892:331). The blades are lanceolate in shape with a slight ridge running down the middle on both sides. Figure 99 shows the double-bladed paddles used by two kayakers off Icy Cape just south of Wainright.

Figure 98. North Alaska style kayak model on sled. 1960s. Length 16". Collection Alaska State Museum. II-A-4623.

Figure 99. Kayakers at Icy Cape, Alaska, August 1923. Photograph courtesy of the Public Archives of Canada.

Capsize

Apparently, capsizes were not uncommon. At a post-hunt dance, all those who had capsized during the hunt were required to dance *"that they may shake off the salt water, where the beluga had been, from their bodies"* (Curtis 1930 Vol. 20:164). It was said that a capsize was caused by digging the double-bladed paddle too deep in the water.

Paddling Techniques

Both single and double-bladed paddles were used. The double was especially useful when speed was necessary as, for example, in hunting caribou. A double-bladed paddle collected at Point Barrow in 1883 measured 7 feet long with the shaft having

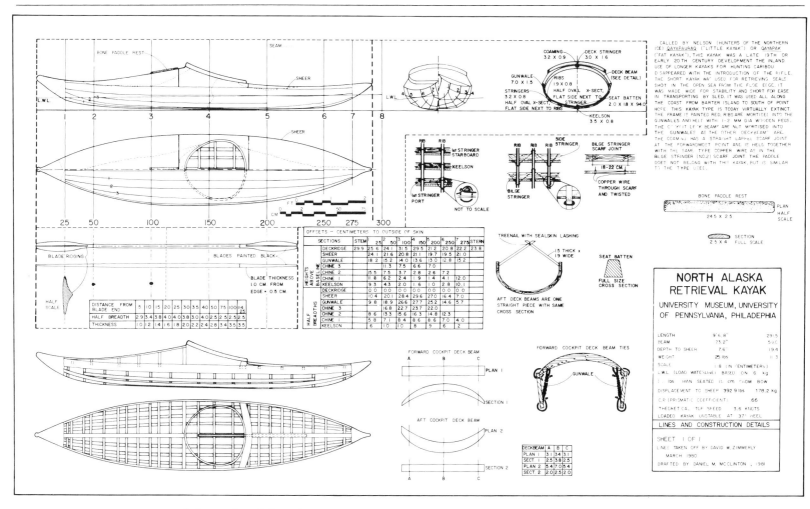

Figure 100. Lines and construction details of a North Alaska retrieval kayak. Length 9' 6.8". University of Pennsylvania Museum, Philadelphia. Sheet (1 of 1). Line drawing IV-E-24M © Canadian Museum of Civilization.

North Alaska Retrieval Kayak

This short, relatively wide kayak was a late 19th or early 20th century development. It was called a **qayapauraq,** little kayak, or **qayapak,** fat kayak (Nelson 1966:307). Figure 100 is a good example of the type. Richard Nelson's mid-1960s informants said this kayak was 9 to 12 feet long, 24 to 30 inches wide, and 35 to 40 pounds (1969:287).

The inland use of the longer Kotzebue/Point Barrow style of kayak disappeared with the introduction of the rifle. Caribou could be easily shot from a distance without a kayak. Seals could be shot from the floe edge, but some sort of craft was necessary to retrieve them. The shortened kayak was developed just for this task.

The retrieval kayak was made wide for stability and short for ease in transporting by sled. It was used all along the coast from Barter Island near the

Canadian border to south of Point Hope. Wainwright hunter, Nashoalook, told Richard Nelson, *"...that by the 1920's [sic] the long types were no longer in existence and virtually every man had his own retrieving kayak. Since that time they have declined steadily, following the introduction of the very safe and utilitarian umiahaluraq, or small umiaq"(1966:239).* This kayak type is virtually extinct today.

The kayak in Figure 100 has a red-painted frame. The ribs are mortised into the gunwales and held with wooden pegs. The cockpit deck beams are not mortised into the gunwales as the other deckbeams are. Construction is similar to other

North Alaska kayak types. Figure 102 is an inside view of this kayak looking forward. Note the two-piece deck beams instead of the naturally-curved types use in the Bering Strait and Bering Sea areas. Note also the lashing that fastens the ribs to the longitudinal stringers. They are tied from bow to stern instead of in the southern method of gunwale to gunwale. There is an extra batten on top of part of the keelson used to give added strength in the cockpit area. The skin covering was usually bearded seal.

Figure 101 shows a retrieval kayak in use, but the paddle seems to be the broad-bladed Copper Eskimo type instead of the normal paddle as shown in Figure 100.

Figure 102. Interior view of North Alaska retrieval kayak specimen detailed in Fig. 100. Collection University Museum, University of Pennsylvania, Philadelphia.

Figure 101. North Alaska retrieval kayak in Camden Bay, Alaska, just west of Barter Island. Photograph by R. M. Anderson of the 1913-1916 Canadian Arctic Expedition, courtesy of the National Museums of Canada.

Figure 103. Nunamiut kayak frame made by Simon Paneak in 1972 for the University of Alaska Museum. Photograph courtesy of University of Alaska Museum.

Nunamiut

Another subtype of North Alaska inland kayaks was found in the Brooks Range area where the Nunamiut Eskimo lived. The mainstay of the Nunamiut was the caribou which migrated yearly in great herds to and from the sea. Anaktuvuk Pass was a natural funnel through which the animals passed. An efficient method of hunting was to drive them into a lake or ambush them at a river crossing where they could be speared from a kayak.

Taking Off Lines

A simple, but very effective technique for measuring cross sections was taught to me by kayak researcher John Heath.

First, measure the beam at the cross section station. Traditionally, boats were evenly divided into ten cross section stations. Modern mathematical methods and computers have removed this restriction. I find it convenient to mark sections first at 25 cm from the bow, then at 50 cm and then every 50 cm until the last station, which should be near to 25 cm from the stern.

Next, wrap a piece of heavy gauge solder tightly around the hull up to the gunwales on both sides. Use a marking pen to put marks on the solder where any chines are located. Carefully remove the solder from the kayak and lay it on a piece of paper. Position the solder so that the parts that bend inward at the gunwales are placed on the paper at the premeasured beam distance. This will force the rest of the solder to conform to the cross section and a line may be traced around the inside of the solder for a perfect record of the cross section.

Spearing Caribou

Nicholas Gubser lived with the Nunamiut during 1960-61 and described the method of hunting caribou from a kayak.

When a hunter paddled near the swimming caribou, he had to be very careful to spear the animal high in the rib cage just to one side of the backbone, puncturing either the heart or the lungs, so that the caribou would die quietly. He had to learn to jab the spear in very smartly.and withdraw it just as quickly so that the animal would not overturn the kayak. If a beginner jabbed a caribou in the gut, it would thrash violently, possibly upsetting him, and very few Nunamiut can swim. Sometimes, when the caribou were crowded together, a kayaker might literally be borne along on the backs of the herd, stabbing caribou right and left. The last Nunamiut kayak was made during World War II, when ammunition ran short. The Nunamiut who used it said it was easy to kill a very large number of caribou. In the old days, several men in kayaks could kill all a band could possibly consume in a winter, sometimes more caribou than the whole community could skin and butcher, provided, of course, that sufficient caribou were to be had (Gubser 1965:176).

69

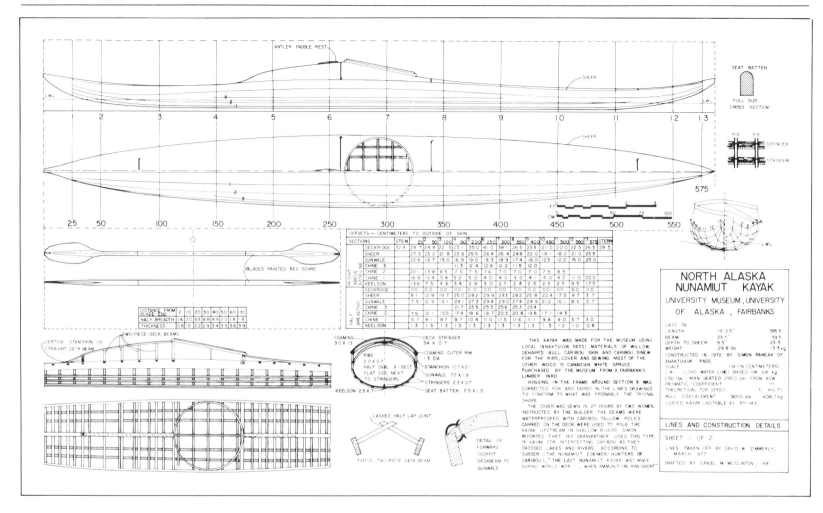

Kayak Construction

Figure 104 illustrates the only existing museum specimen of a Nunamiut kayak. It is a bit longer, but somewhat narrower than the average Kotzebue/Point Barrow inland kayak. The major difference is that while there is reverse sheer at the cockpit area, both bow and stern curve upwards. This specimen was made for the University of Alaska Museum by the late Simon Paneak, a respected Nunamiut, who seems to have been everyone's favorite informant for Nunamiut cultural information.

The kayak was made at the museum in 1972 using willow, bull caribou skin and sinew from Anaktuvuk Pass and Canadian white spruce from a Fairbanks lumber yard. The caribou hide cover was sewn in 27 hours by two women who were instructed by the builder. Seams were waterproofed with caribou tallow. The completed kayak weighs only 29.8 pounds and is stable with a kayaker in it up to 51 degrees of heel. Figure 103 shows the completed kayak frame just before covering.

Figure 104. Lines and construction details of a North Alaska Nunamiut kayak constructed in 1972 by Simon Paneak of Anaktuvuk Pass. Length 19' 2.5". University of Alaska Museum, Fairbanks. Sheet (1 of 2). Line drawing IV-E-21M © Canadian Museum of Civilization.

By geographical definition, the Mackenzie Eskimo kayak is grouped with Canadian Inuit kayaks. However, by type it is more closely related to some Alaska kayaks, and should be included in this survey. Indeed, it is the kayak characteristics, along with other archaeological evidence, that suggests the Mackenzie Eskimo group migrated from western Alaska at least 500 years ago (McGhee 1972:92–93).

The group inhabited the muddy delta, rich in resources, where the Mackenzie River breaks up into myriad channels as it flows into the Beaufort Sea. Their kayaks were markedly different from those of the Kotzebue Sound/Point Barrow area to the west or the crude Copper Eskimo kayak to the east. The ridged deck, upswept bow and rounded bottom are

reminiscent of King Island kayaks. The craftsmanship is superb.

Sustained European contact with the Mackenzie Eskimos began in the mid-1800s with the establishment of trading posts in the area. Descriptions of the groups living in the delta come from those traders, early explorers, and a few survivors. The group was culturally extinct by 1910.

Kayak Use

The Mackenzie Inuit used their kayaks for hunting whales and seals, setting and hauling fishnets, and spearing caribou in inland lakes. The most spectacular use was in the communal beluga whale

Figure 104a. Lines and construction sections of a classic Mackenzie Eskimo kayak. Length 16′ 5″. Line drawing of museum specimen NMM IV-D-2039, National Museums of Canada.

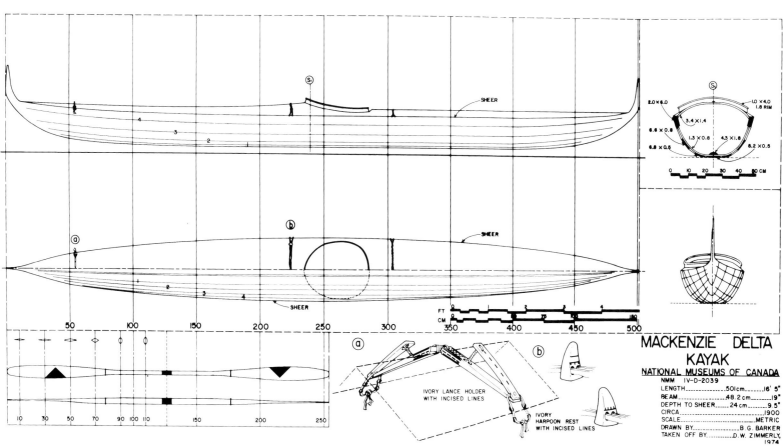

MACKENZIE DELTA KAYAK
NATIONAL MUSEUMS OF CANADA
NMM IV-D-2039
LENGTH............................501cm................16′ 5″
BEAM................................48.2 cm..............19″
DEPTH TO SHEER.......24 cm.............9.5″
CIRCA...1900
SCALE..METRIC
DRAWN BY.........................B.G. BARKER
TAKEN OFF BY...........D.W. ZIMMERLY
1974

hunts that took place between mid-July and early September. Local tradition suggests that two hundred kayaks might have been the normal number engaged in large hunts (McGhee 1974:19).

Imagine two hundred kayaks being launched, one by one from a sandbank until they form a single line five miles long. Such a hunt was described by Nuligak, born in 1895 and just a boy at the time of the last great hunts.

The first among my early memories is of the white whale hunt. In the spring the families from all the surrounding camps came to Kitigariuit for the hunt. Lots of people—lots of kayaks. I was too young to be able to count them; I only know the long sandbank of Kitigariuit beach was hardly long enough for all the kayaks drawn up there. And the beach was a good eight or nine hundred yards long. The sight of all those kayaks putting out to sea was a spectacle we children never tired of.

When the kayak fleet first assembled, a file leader was chosen by the hunters…. It was he who launched the first kayak in pursuit of the whales once they were among the shoals…. The chosen hunter's kayak would be followed by a second, a third, and the others in succession…. I remember there was such a large number of kayaks that when the first had disappeared from view more and more were just setting out (Nuligak 1966:14–15).

The kayaks were setting a whale trap. During the short summer, the Mackenzie estuary is a rich feeding ground for fish. The beluga whales came into the shoal water in search of fish and were, in turn, hunted by the Inuit.

The hunters, paddling with all their might, drove their craft in pursuit of the whales. Then, on the seaward side of the shallows, they faced the belugas and paddled forward, all abreast. With loud shouts they struck the water with their

paddles, splashing it in great cascades. Panic-stricken at the noise, the whales threw themselves on the sandbanks in their efforts to flee. The largest soon had but two feet of water beneath them and found it impossible to escape (ibid.:14–15).

The ensuing slaughter supplied the Inuit with meat and blubber for the long winter.

When the hunt was over, the men recovered their weapons. Each harpoon bore a special mark, recognized by every hunter. Clever hunters might have killed five, seven belugas, while others had taken but one. To haul the whales back to camp, a sort of pipe was driven into their bodies or necks, and air was blown

Figure 104b. Mackenzie Eskimo kayaks with one man paddling with a broken paddle, 1901, at Fort McPherson on the Peel River (Mathers 1972:15). Photograph by C. W. Mathers. Courtesy of the Public Archives of Canada.

into the carcasses so they would float. A single man often had as many as five belugas in tow behind his kayak.

After a hunt the shore was covered with whale carcasses. For myself, I did not count them, but I know there were a great many. Once I heard the elders say that three hundred whales had been taken. At other times there were but one hundred and fifty of them. There are not many belugas any more. The Inuit scarcely see any during their expeditions — the Inuit eat white man's food nowadays (ibid.:14–15).

British Officer Alexander Armstrong reported that those who killed the whales were honored by tattooing "with one line extending outwards from the inner angle of the eye across the cheek; for each one taken, the captor became entitled to an additional mark" (1857:176).

Mackenzie Eskimo History

The Mackenzie Eskimos were extremely successful, by far the largest Inuit group in Canada. Based on the number of people encountered by various explorers throughout the coastal area, it is estimated

Figure 104c. "Kookpugmioot Eskimos"—Mackenzie Eskimos. The upward projecting pieces at bow and stern of the kayaks are for hauling them over ice. Photograph courtesy of the Peabody Museum, Cambridge.

that a minimum of 2500 Inuit occupied the delta around 1850 (McGhee 1974:7). Yet by 1910, their numbers had dwindled to a mere 150 souls. Europeans inadvertently introduced epidemics of scarlet fever, influenza, small pox, and measles. The American whaling fleet appeared along the Mackenzie Delta coast in 1889. The increased association of the Native population with whalers wintering over in the area accelerated the cultural decline. Two devastating measles epidemics in 1900 and 1902 further decimated the population. The remnants of their culture were lost as western Alaska Inuit absorbed the surviving members.

Museum Examples

To my knowledge, only five of their many kayaks remain in museum collections. One (DNM P31:61) was collected in 1924 for the Danish National Museum in Copenhagen by the famous Danish explorer Knud Rasmussen. It was said to be the last kayak to be found in the Mackenzie area. National Museum of Canada ethnologist Diamond Jenness collected two small Mackenzie kayaks (IV-D-1058 and IV-D-2002) during the 1913–16 Canadian Arctic Expedition. Adney and Chapelle illustrate one from the Museum of the American Indian, Heye Foundation (1964:201, fig.188).

In the mid-1970s, while I was arctic ethnologist at the National Museum of Man (now the Canadian Museum of Civilization) I collected a Mackenzie Eskimo kayak through an art dealer. It was said to have hung for years on the wall of an English castle. Of the few examples, this kayak best represents the type seen in early photographs, and is the one illustrated here.

Kayak Construction

The 16'5" Mackenzie Eskimo kayak (fig. 104a) is decked, full-ended, narrow-beamed (19"), rounded, multichined, and covered with sealskin. It has a straight bottom and rising bow and stern that terminate in two vertical horns. There is little sheer

except for a slight amount near the bow (Zimmerly 1985:7–10).

The craftsmanship in this example exceeds that of any examples in North Alaska and Canada. It is equivalent to that from Nome south in Alaska including the Aleutians.

The cockpit coaming is slightly raked and rests fore and aft on curved deck beams of somewhat heavier construction than the other deck beams. The coaming is of the floating type with the skin covering under it.

The deck is slightly ridged along its full length due to a high narrow deck stringer whose top surface is above the deckline.

The keelson, bilge stringers, and side stringers (one on each side) are unusual in being very wide and so thin that they curve under the force of the cover to

Figure 104d. Museum specimen NMM IV-D-1058 showing the wide, flat, curved stringers, and the half-round batten under the seat. Photograph by David W. Zimmerly. Courtesy of the Canadian Museum of Civilization.

74

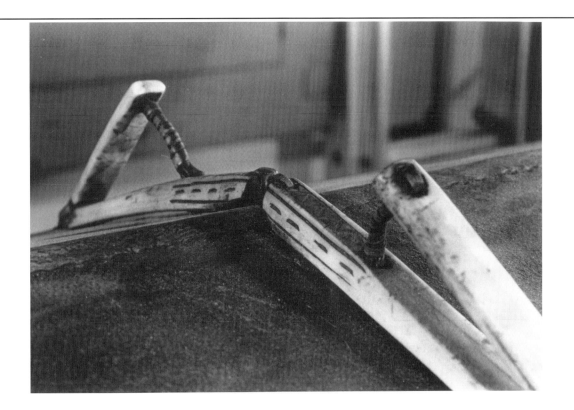

give an almost truly round hull. A small half-round batten is fastened longitudinally across the ribs down the centerline of the keelson and extends only a short distance fore and aft of the cockpit to provide added support for the thin keelson to prevent sagging.

Framework lashings are of baleen, sinew, and some type of root, probably spruce. The slight craft weighs only 32 pounds.

Accessories

Nuligak provided a description of the accessories taken on the whale hunt.

The kayak paddles bore designs in red, and the hunters' weapons were red as well. Each kayak was furnished with two harpoons of very slender wood, eight or nine feet long. To one of the harpoons was attached a kind of skin bottle, rather small and inflated with air. A long string was tied to the end of the second harpoon. A wooden disc, illiviark, was fastened to the middle of the string, and at the end was another skin bag, larger than that of the first harpoon, and embellished by eagle feathers. The kayak itself was sixteen to eighteen feet long, eighteen or nineteen inches wide, and about fourteen inches deep. The two harpoons were in their place on the foredeck (ibid.:14–15).

There are very few extant Mackenzie Eskimo kayak accessories. The kayak illustrated in figure 1 came with a double-bladed paddle. The 8'3 $\frac{3}{4}$" paddle has narrow (4") lanceolate-shaped blades although the tips are rounded somewhat. There is slight ridging on both sides of the blades; the shaft is oval with the widest part perpendicular to the plane of the blades. Drip rings are slight in cross-section with one made of braided sinew and the other of baleen. The paddle is painted with a red ochre color in a bank around the middle and in a triangular pattern on both sides of both blades (Zimmerly 1984:12–13).

This is a superb paddle, well-balanced, and powerful. My white pine replica remained my favorite paddle for years.

Special deck loops were placed far forward where lances could be secured. A hunter, depending on the game he sought, might carry several types of harpoons, a bird spear, extra paddle, and a small stick one to two feet in length with a hook on the end used to push and pull stowed gear from and to the cockpit.

Armstrong was a surgeon with H.M.S. *Investigator* in search of the Franklin Expedition. In 1857 he wrote about meeting some eastern Mackenzie Eskimos. Two Eskimos in their kayaks were hoisted aboard. In searching for a leak one of the Eskimos emptied his kayak giving Armstrong "an opportunity of seeing how well they were stocked, including spare materials to repair any disaster that boat or implements might sustain" (page 186). Later Armstrong reported that:

The owner of the leaky kayak, as soon as his countrywomen came on board, seized one of them and pointed out to her the hole in it. She immediately procured a needle from him and thread of reindeer tendon; and, with great quickness and cheerfulness, set about the repair, which she quickly accomplished. I naturally assumed she was his wife; but such was not the case, as I found on inquiring (page 188).

Skin Coverings

Sewing the skin kayak covers was women's work all across the Arctic. The task was demanding, requiring great skill in the preparation, cutting, fitting, and meticulous joining of the skins to provide a tight-fitting, waterproof covering. The seam was double sewn. The first seam joined the skins. The second, stitched only through the inner layers, made the seam waterproof. The joint responsibility of building a kayak is a prime example of the symbiotic nature of male/female roles in traditional Eskimo culture. The hunter could not be successful without a wife skilled in sewing the necessay skin clothing and kayak covering.

Siberian and Alaskan Kayak Paddle-Type Distribution

	Blade Length			Blade Shape		Bone on Blade Edge or Tips	Drip Ring	Average Length (inches)	Average Length (cm)	Average Max. Width (inches)	Average Max. Width (cm)
	Long	Medium	Short	Symmetrical	Non-symmetrical						
Koryak single			•	•		•		16.5	41.9	4.75	12.1
double	Type Reported — No Data Available										
Chukchi single	•			•				65.8	167.0	3.9	10.0
double			•		•			94.5	240.0	6.8	17.4
Aleut single	•										
double	•				•			96.1	244.4	3.7	9.4
Pacific Eskimo single	•			•				60.7	154.3	4.5	11.5
double	Type Reported — No Data Available										
Bering Sea single	•			•				60.7	154.1	5.3	13.4
double		•						101.7	258.2		
Bering Strait single	•			•				59.8	152.0	5.6	14.2
double		•	•		•			97.3	247.1	2.7	6.8
North Alaska double				•	•	•		84.6	215.0	3.6	9.1

All Arctic kayak paddles may be conveniently divided into two main types, single-bladed and double-bladed. They can be further classified according to blade length, blade shape, blade symmetry and the use or non-use of bone tips, bone edging and drip rings.

The single-bladed paddles (always with symmetric blades) are found in use among the Koryak, Chukchi, Aleut, Kodiak, Bering Sea, Bering Strait and Mackenzie Delta peoples. Double-bladed paddles were used everywhere. Both symmetric and non-symmetric blades are found on doubles.

The wood most used in paddle-making was black spruce. This tree is commonly found as driftwood on all Arctic beaches. It is the last tree found before the treeline stops and tundra takes over.

The paddles that have non-symmetrical blades are flat or slightly convex on one side and ridged on the other. The ridging strengthens the blade and prevents blade "chatter."

Paddle length was partly determined by kayak size. A deep wide kayak needed a single-bladed paddle or an extremely long double. Because the elbows had to be held high to clear the cockpit, the double-bladed paddle was very tiring to use. It became too heavy and cumbersome and was used only when speed was important.

Figure 105.

Specialized Paddles

Specialized paddles that more closely resembled ping-pong paddles than kayak paddles were developed by the Siberian Koryak (see Figure 106). While the Koryak were reported to have double-bladed paddles, I have only seen the small lanyard-attached paddles as in the illustration.

The Siberian Chukchi used single-bladed paddles in the sea (Nordenskiold 1881:93) and double-bladed ones for use in reindeer hunting in inland lakes and rivers. The doubles (Figure 107) had short wide blades with a knife or lance head lashed to the tip of one blade. While pursuing reindeer, which swim at speeds to 5 knots, a Chukchi hunter could quickly change from paddling to thrusting his paddle/lance into the rib cage of the fleeing animal.

Another specialized paddle was developed by Bering Sea kayakers. Symmetrically-bladed, it was just over two feet in length and 3.5 inches in width and included a small hand grip. It was used to control the kayak during the final approach toward a sleepy seal sunning himself on an icefloe. This strange paddle was grasped, as one would a walking stick, in one hand while the other held a harpoon at the ready. The paddle was maneuvered in

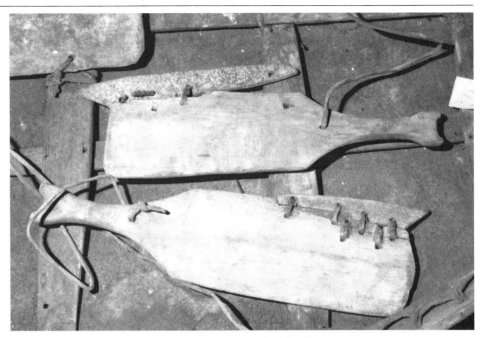

Figure 106. Koryak hand paddles from a Koryak kayak. The purpose of the bone on the paddles is unknown. Perhaps it served as an ice scraper. Collection American Museum of Natural History. AMNH 70/3358.

Figure 107. Inland Siberian Chukchi paddle with spear on end for lancing swimming caribou. Measurements are in centimeters.

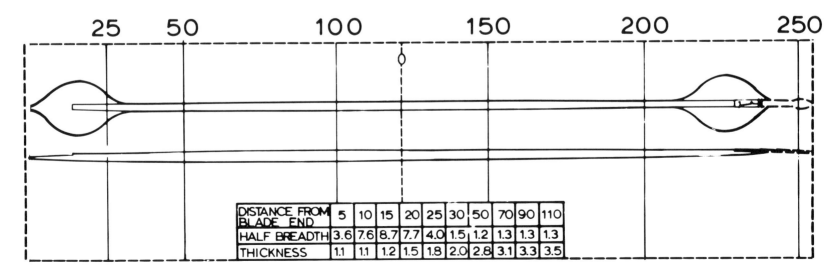

DISTANCE FROM BLADE END	5	10	15	20	25	30	50	70	90	110
HALF BREADTH	3.6	7.6	8.7	7.7	4.0	1.5	1.2	1.3	1.3	1.3
THICKNESS	1.1	1.1	1.2	1.5	1.8	2.0	2.8	3.1	3.3	3.5

a sculling motion without taking it out of the water. This prevented dripping water noises waking up the seal.

Aleut Paddles

The average Aleut double-bladed paddle has a length of about 8 feet (244.4 cm) with a width of just under 4 inches (9.4 cm). These paddles have long non-symmetric blades. Figure 109 illustrates a typical Aleut double-bladed paddle. The blade cross section shows one side slightly convex, tending toward the flat, with the other side ridged the full length for strength. This paddle has red blades and a black shaft, while others are decorated with black shaft and natural blades. Other variations are red tip, black blade and red shaft with black ring around the middle; and red tips, blue blades and red shaft.

The Aleut also had single-bladed paddles carried as spares.

Figure 108. Special hand paddle made by Dick Bunyan in Hooper Bay, Alaska, 1977.

Figure 109. Aleut double-bladed paddle from Unalaska. Collection Smithsonian Institution. USNM 76281.

Pacific Eskimo Paddles

Alaska's Kodiak and Chugach Eskimo had similar kayaks and paddles. They normally used long, narrow, lance shaped single-bladed paddles with

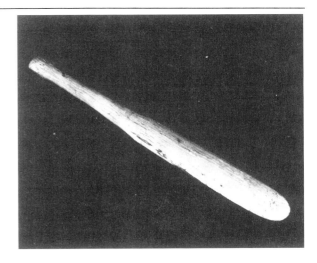

symmetric blades. Kodiak paddle blades were invariably painted red and black with the shafts left natural. Chugach paddles sometimes had green blades.

Double-bladed paddles are found on models of Pacific Eskimo kayaks, but I have not seen any full size ones. They were used when great speed was wanted, while hunting sea-otters for example.

Figure 110 shows three typical Kodiak Eskimo paddles. They are in the collections of the Museum of Anthropology and Ethnography in Leningrad and were collected by Yury Lisiansky about 1805. The blades of all three are symmetrically ridged with edge thickness varying from about 1/8 inch (0.3 cm) at the tip to 1/8 inch—1/4 inch (0.4—0.6 cm) at the sides extending almost to the loom.

Bering Sea Paddles

The Bering Sea people (Bristol Bay, Nunivak Island, the Kuskokwim/Yukon Delta region and Norton Sound) used double-bladed paddles for speed and singles for normal use. After the introduction of rifles, the kayaks became beamier for greater

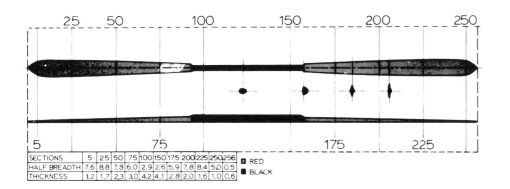

SECTIONS	5	25	50	75	100	150	175	200	225	250	256
HALF BREADTH	7.6	8.8	7.3	6.0	2.9	2.6	5.9	7.8	8.4	5.0	0.5
THICKNESS	1.2	1.7	2.3	3.0	4.2	4.1	2.8	2.0	1.6	1.0	0.6

■ RED
■ BLACK

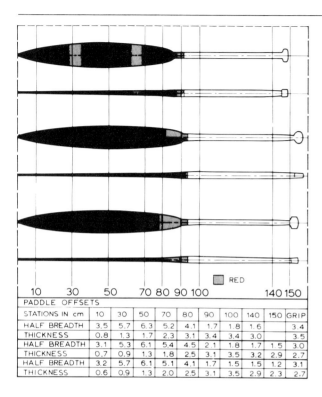

PADDLE OFFSETS									
STATIONS IN cm	10	30	50	70	80	90	100	140	150	GRIP
HALF BREADTH	3.5	5.7	6.3	5.2	4.1	1.7	1.8	1.6		3.4
THICKNESS	0.8	1.3	1.7	2.3	3.1	3.4	3.4	3.0		3.5
HALF BREADTH	3.1	5.3	6.1	5.4	4.5	2.1	1.8	1.7	1.5	3.0
THICKNESS	0.7	0.9	1.3	1.8	2.5	3.1	3.5	3.2	2.9	2.7
HALF BREADTH	3.2	5.7	6.1	5.1	4.1	1.7	1.5	1.5	1.2	3.1
THICKNESS	0.6	0.9	1.3	2.0	2.5	3.1	3.5	2.9	2.3	2.7

cm) diameter with the diameter measuring 1½ inches (3.7 cm) in the middle. The blade is painted blue with the shaft and grip green.

Kayak builder Dick Bunyan told me that the correct paddle length for Hooper Bay kayaks is an arm span (the original measure for a fathom) with the ends gripped in the second finger-joints.

Figure 110. Kodiak Eskimo paddles in the collections of the Museum of Anthropology and Ethnography in Leningrad were collected around 1805.

Figure 111. King Island style kayak paddle collected in 1878 by A.E. Nordenskiold in Port Clarence, Alaska.

stability and the use of the double-bladed paddle went almost out of existence. I saw none in use in the Bering Sea area in the mid-1970s.

The single-bladed paddles average about 5 feet (154.1 cm) in overall length with blades less than half the total paddle length and a "T" grip put on with a mortise and tenon joint. Painting of shaft and blade was common.

Figure 112 is a Bristol Bay type single-bladed paddle in the collections of the Alaska State Museum. It is similar to a single-bladed paddle which I collected in Hooper Bay in 1976. The blade of the Hooper Bay paddle is ridged symmetrically on both sides with the blade cross section concave from the ridge to the blade edge. The shaft has a round cross section. The blade is ¼ inch (0.6 cm) thick at a distance of 3/16 inch (0.5 cm) from the edge. The grip ends are 1 inch (2.6

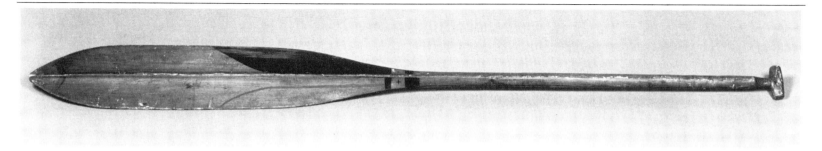

Photograph by Mark Daughhetee

Bering Strait Paddles

Figure 112. Bristol Bay style paddle. Collection Alaska State Museum. III-A-3671.

Figure 113. North Alaska retrieval kayak paddle.

Bering Strait paddles exhibit the greatest variability of any group discussed. There are few examples of double-bladed paddles. The singles have long symmetric blades with the handgrips often carved rather than mortised on.

The King Island variety of Bering Strait paddles have the most elaborate painted decorations on the blades. The paint was usually black and red. Some of these paddles are further decorated with grooves

carved up the side starting where the blade joins the loom. Paddle length was determined exactly the same as in Hooper Bay. The loom was elliptical in cross section with the maximum diameter perpendicular to the plane of the blade.

According to John Heath's informants the double-bladed paddle (pautik) was one and one-half arm-spans long with blades about 20 inches (50.8 cm) long by 4 inches (10.2 cm) wide. The loom was elliptical (1972:26).

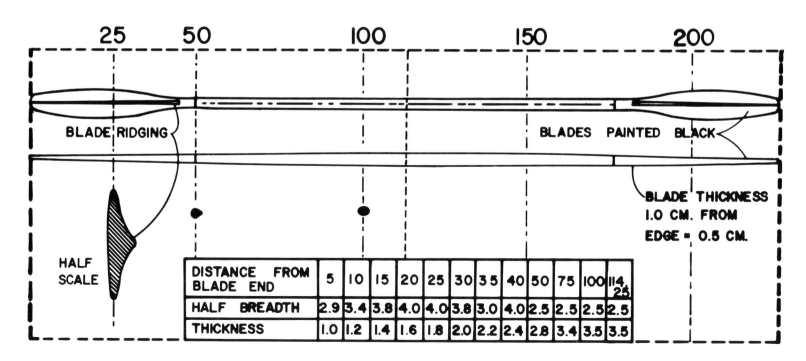

BLADE RIDGING

BLADES PAINTED BLACK

BLADE THICKNESS 1.0 CM. FROM EDGE = 0.5 CM.

HALF SCALE

DISTANCE FROM BLADE END	5	10	15	20	25	30	35	40	50	75	100	114.25
HALF BREADTH	2.9	3.4	3.8	4.0	4.0	3.8	3.0	4.0	2.5	2.5	2.5	2.5
THICKNESS	1.0	1.2	1.4	1.6	1.8	2.0	2.2	2.4	2.8	3.4	3.5	3.5

North Alaska Paddles

Paddles of North Alaska are all double-bladed with short blades that may or may not be symmetric. Usually they were ridged on at least one side. Red and black paint on blades, shaft or both was not uncommon.

Figure 113 is of a typical North Alaska double-bladed paddle. It is in the collections of the University Museum at the University of Pennsylvania. Unfortunately there is no date or prove-nience listed, but it was associated with a short kayak of the type used for retrieving seals shot from the floe edge. The black-painted blades are ridged on one side only. The shaft has an elliptical cross section.

Figure 114 illustrates a North Alaska inland Nunamiut kayak paddle. The paddle has red ocher painted blades ridged on both sides with round cross sectional shaft.

Figure 114. Nunamiut inland kayak paddle.

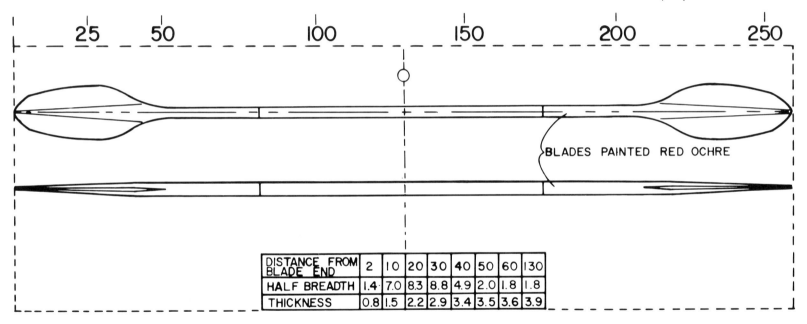

BLADES PAINTED RED OCHRE

DISTANCE FROM BLADE END	2	10	20	30	40	50	60	130
HALF BREADTH	1.4	7.0	8.3	8.8	4.9	2.0	1.8	1.8
THICKNESS	0.8	1.5	2.2	2.9	3.4	3.5	3.6	3.9

CONCLUSIONS

Today, much of the technology and culture surrounding Arctic kayaks is already lost, while that which remains is in imminent danger of being forgotten. Perhaps this exhibition and book, will foster renewed interest in historic kayak designs.

By understanding the Arctic roots of contemporary fiberglass kayaks, we can combine innovative features and designs from the past with new materials from the present to create a superior craft. Kayak builders from Greenland, Canada and Alaska all adapted different designs to meet their particular needs for stealth, seaworthiness and carrying capacity. Today's ocean paddlers can do the same.

The modern sport of sea kayaking has flourished only since the start of this decade. It is a relatively inexpensive sport, it is environmentally clean and it provides a means of travel to the far corners of the world. Clubs, magazines and manufacturers have sprung up all over North America and Europe. Sea kayaking is a wonderful way to preserve the past. Better yet—we can experience the past by silently paddling a craft that was designed to perfection over 4,000 years ago.

Figure 115. The traditional skin covered kayak has evolved into a streamlined recreational craft. A modern fiberglass VCP Selkie kayak and quill paddle is demonstrated by Ron Ripple, courtesy of Alaska Discovery.

Photograph by Paul Gardinier

APRON A waterproof cloth used to keep water out of the cockpit. It fastens around the coaming and the paddler's waist. Also called spray apron, white water skirt, or spraydeck.

BAIDARKA, BIDARKA Term used originally by Russians for the decked skin-covered kayak. In southern Alaska the spelling is usually BIDARKI or BIDARKY, a corruption of the Russian plural BAIDARKI.

CANOE Traditionally a non-decked long and narrow boat, sharp at both ends, with curved sides, usually built of lightweight materials and propelled by a kneeling paddler using a single-bladed paddle.

CHINE Any corner or angle as opposed to a curve in a cross section. A hard chine is one over 45 degrees.

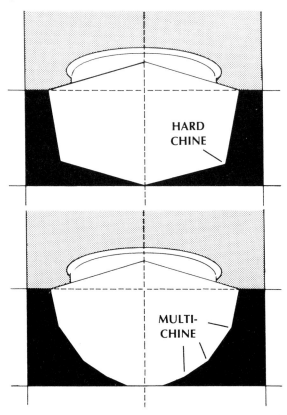

HARD CHINE

MULTI-CHINE

COAMING A raised, usually vertical, framing around cockpit to keep water out. Used interchangeably with hoop or cockpit hoop. Kayak coamings are sometimes an integral part of the framework (fixed coaming) with the skin covering fastened over them, or they may be the floating type where they only rest against the fore and aft cockpit deck beams and are held in place by the skin covering which comes under them.

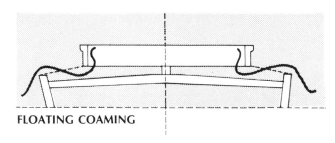

FLOATING COAMING

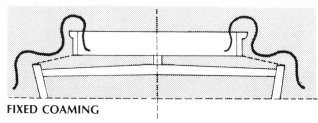

FIXED COAMING

COCKPIT An opening in the deck for the paddler.

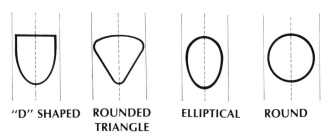

"D" SHAPED   ROUNDED TRIANGLE   ELLIPTICAL   ROUND

DEADRISE The angle at which the bottom rises from where it joins the keel to the turn of the bilge, or chine. An angle more than 20 degrees, called steep deadrise, is typical for boats designed for heavy seas.

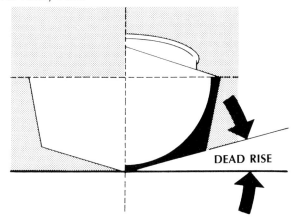

DECK. The top covering of kayak extending from side to side (gunwale to gunwale). Kayaks have either flat decks or ridged decks.

DECK SHAPES

FLAT   RIDGED

DECK BEAM An athwartships member that spreads the gunwales. Used interchangeably with cross beam and thwart although the latter technically refers to a crosswise seat in a small open boat.

DECK LINE Athwartships line usually fore and aft of the cockpit, used to secure various hunting implements.

DEPTH A measurement of inside hull roominess. Measured at the point of maximum beam from the outside hull center up to the sheer line (sometimes recorded as depth to sheer). Depth is the most unstandardized measurement used in regard to kayaks, making comparisons between types difficult. The above measurement is the recommended one.

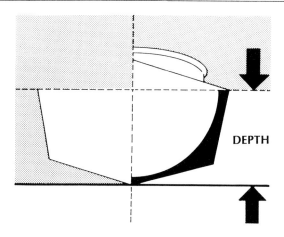

DIRECTIONAL STABILITY A measurement of a craft's ability to maintain a straight line movement despite cross winds, uneven paddling, etc., an important feature in a craft designed for hunting sea mammals. Right before shooting or harpooning a seal, the hunter must stop paddling. A craft with poor directional stability could veer off course, ruining the hunter's aim. A craft with a high degree of directional stability will be less maneuverable than one without. Directional stability and maneuverability are inversely proportional to each other. **See also STABILITY.**

DRAFT, DRAUGHT The depth a craft sinks in water.

DRIP RING A rubber collar, braided sinew or seal skin band, or wooden protuberance between the blades and hand grips of a double-bladed paddle that prevents water from running down the shaft onto the paddler's hands. **See also PADDLE.**

FLARE Outward spread and upward curve of the topsides as they rise from the waterline, most noticeably in the bow sections. While a kayak's skin cover can only form a concave curve under special circumstances, the term flare is used to describe the usual non-vertical sides. There is no standardized degree of angle of flare to define slightly flared, moderately flared and sharply flared. **See also HULL.**

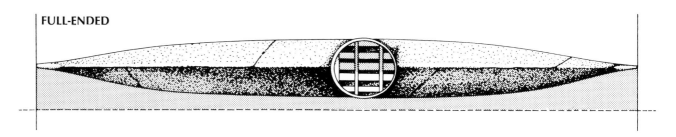

FULL-ENDED

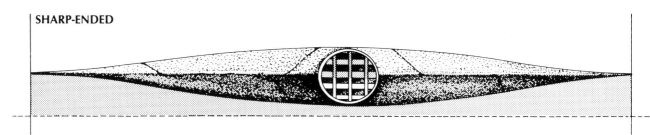

SHARP-ENDED

HULL SHAPES

FLAT BOTTOM

**STRAIGHT SIDES
HARD CHINE**

V BOTTOM

ROUND BOTTOM

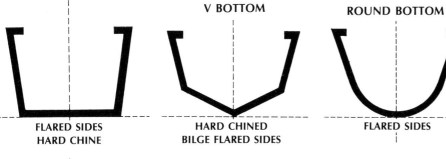

**FLARED SIDES
HARD CHINE**

**HARD CHINED
BILGE FLARED SIDES**

FLARED SIDES

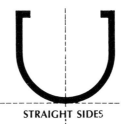

**FLARED SIDES
ROUNDED BILGE**

**ROUNDED BILGE
FLARED SIDES**

STRAIGHT SIDES

FULL-ENDED A craft that maintains a fairly wide beam almost to the stem as opposed to one that tapers gradually to sharp ends and is termed sharp-ended.

GUNWALE The upper edge of sides of a craft. The uppermost wale of a ship, next below the bulwarks. So called because guns were set upon it. In kayaks, it refers to the deep uppermost longitudinal stringer that is the main strength member in the framework.

HULL The basic structural shell of a craft. Kayaks are of three basic types: flat-bottomed, V-bottomed and round-bottomed with several variations of each type. With the exception of the Mackenzie kayak, all other round bottom types are actually multi-chine hulls.

KEEL The bottom outside center support of a craft. True arctic kayaks had a keelson instead of a keel. **See also KEELSON.**

KEELSON The bottom centerline longtitudinal strength member inside a kayak. As all parts of a kayaks framework are contained inside the skin cover, there can be no true keel.

MANEUVERABILITY A relative measure of how easily a kayak can execute a turn. **See also DIRECTIONAL STABILITY.**

MULTI-CHINE A multi-chine hull is one with a series of hard angles instead of a smoothly curved surface. Traditional Arctic kayaks with hulls termed round are actually multi-chined due to the properties of the stretched skin cover.

RIB One of the curved timbers or members in a craft's frame which spring upward and outward from the keel (keelson in a kayak) area. Used interchangeably with frame. A rib may be round or bent to a hard angle to form the turn of the bilge.

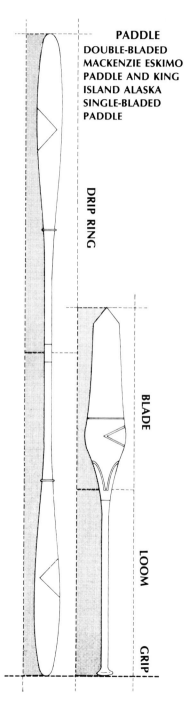

**PADDLE
DOUBLE-BLADED
MACKENZIE ESKIMO
PADDLE AND KING
ISLAND ALASKA
SINGLE-BLADED
PADDLE**

DRIP RING

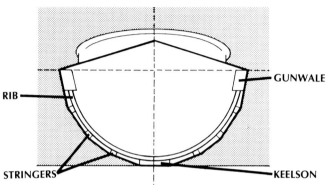

GUNWALE

RIB

STRINGERS

KEELSON

MULTI-CHINE SECTION SHOWING RIBS, STRINGERS, KEELSON AND GUNWALE.

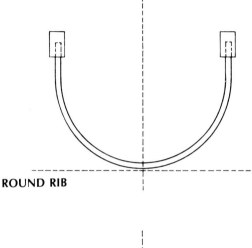

ROUND RIB

PADDLE An oar held in the hands and used for propelling the kayak. Paddles may be single-bladed or double-bladed. The latter type are sometimes equipped with carved hand grips and drip rings. Arctic double-bladed paddles usually have narrow blades that are in the same plane. The blade tips and ends are sometimes strengthened with pegged-on pieces of bone, antler or ivory.

RAKE Inclinization or slope away from the perpendicular or the horizontal. Rake is thought of in a forward to aft sense; thus a cockpit coaming with after edge lower than forward edge is said to be raked. Rake is more often associated with a hard angle while rise connotes an upward curve, especially when describing a bow configuration.

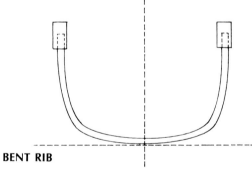

BENT RIB

BLADE

LOOM

GRIP

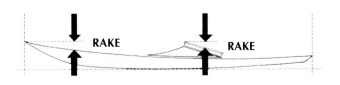

RAKE   RAKE

ROCKER A vertical or upward curve built into the keel (keelson in a kayak) line. A craft with this attribute is said to be rocker-bottomed. **See also HULL.**

SHEER The upward, longitudinal curve of a craft's deck or gunwales. A downward longitudinal curve is termed reverse sheer. A craft with no sheer has a longitudinally straight deckline. Sheer is sometimes used to mean sheer line. A craft with a ridged deck may exhibit a hog-back appearance in profile while at the same time maintaining true sheer along the deckline.

HULL PROFILE SHAPE

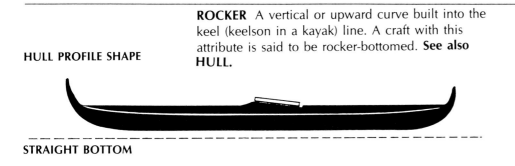

STRAIGHT BOTTOM

ROCKER BOTTOM

DECK PROFILE SHAPE

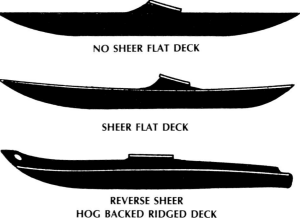

NO SHEER FLAT DECK

SHEER FLAT DECK

REVERSE SHEER
HOG BACKED RIDGED DECK

SCARF JOINT A joint by which the ends of two timbers or the like are fitted with long tapers or laps and glued, nailed, lashed or bolted into a continuous piece.

STRAIGHT SCARF

NOTCHED SCARF

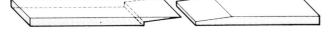

HOOKED SCARF

SLACK BILGE A gentle curved turn of the bilge.

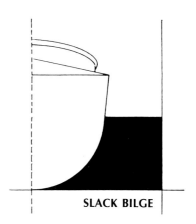

SLACK BILGE

STABILITY The resistance to capsizing or heeling over. A craft's initial stability is that which it has at rest. Final stability is the resistance just before capsizing. V-bottom Greenland kayaks haave good, initial, but poor final stability. The deep, rounded-bottom Bering Sea types with flared sides have poor initial, but good final stability. The Caribou, Netsilik, Copper, Mackenzie and North Alaska types have poor initial and poor final stability.

STRINGER A long horizontal timber connecting upright posts or horizontal timbers. Used interchangeably with batten, lath and strake in reference to a kayak. Special stringers in a kayak are termed: 1. gunwale; 2. keelson; 3. bilge stringer, found at the turn of the bilge; 4. side stringer, one or more of which is found between the gunwale and the bilge stringer; and 5. deck stringer, one or more of which are found on the deck at right angles to the deck beams. Side and bilge stringers on most kayaks are flat or oval in cross-section but are round on many south Alaskan types. If round, they are sometimes called rod battens.

TURN OF THE BILGE The contour where the bottom of a boat meets the topsides. If the intersection of bottom and topsides is formed by a hard angle it is called a hard chine. If it is rounded it is called a rounded turn of the bilge. If it is gently curved it is a slack bilge.

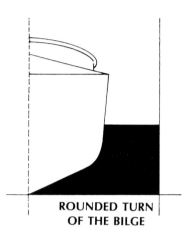

ROUNDED TURN OF THE BILGE

UMIAK An open boat consisting of a wooden frame covered with skins and provided with several thwarts, for transport of goods and passengers and hunting sea mammals.

Adney, Edwin Tappan and Howard I. Chapelle
  1964   THE BARK CANOES AND SKIN BOATS OF NORTH AMERICA.
          Bulletin 230, Smithsonian Institution.

Aigner, Jean S.
  1974   STUDIES IN THE EARLY PREHISTORY OF NIKOLSKI BAY: 1937–
          1971. Anthropological Papers of the University of Alaska, 16(1):9–25.

Antropova, V. V.
  1961   BOATS. Lewis Henry Morgan, trans. (Original: Lodi. In Istoriko-
          etnograficheskii atlas Sibiri. M.G. Levina and L.P. Potapova, eds. Pp.
          107–129. Akademiia Nauk SSSR, Institut etnografii. Lendingrad:
          Izdatyelstvo Akademii nauk SSSR). Unpublished English translation
          (66 typescript pages), Library, National Museums of Canada, Ottawa.

  1971   CULTURE AND EVERYDAY LIFE OF THE KORYAK. (Original: Kultura
          i bytkoryakov. Pp. 33–36. Leningrad: "Nauka" Press). Unpublished
          English translation (16 typescript pages), Library, National Museums
          of Canada, Ottawa.

Armstrong, Alexander
  1857   A PERSONAL NARRATIVE OF THE DISCOVERY OF THE NORTH-
          WEST PASSAGE. London: Hurst & Blackett.

Birket-Smith, Kaj
  1953   THE CHUGACH ESKIMO. NationalmuSeets Skrifter. Etnografisk
          Raekke 6. Copenhagen: NationalmuSeets Publikationsfond.

Black, Lydia T., translator and editor
  1977   THE KONYAG (The Inhabitants of the Island of Kodiak) by Iosaf
          (Bolotov) (1794–1799) and by Gideon (1804–1807). *Arctic
          Anthropology* 14(2):79–108.

Bogoras, Waldemar
  1909   THE CHUKCHEE. Reprinted from Volume 7, Jesup North Pacific
          Expedition, 1904–1909. Memoir 11 American Museum of Natural
          History.

Colnett, Captain J.
  n.d.   "Journal, PRINCE OF WALES, 16 October 1786–7 November 1788."
          Unpublished MS, Admiralty 55/146, Public Record Office, London.

Cook, James and James King
  1785   A VOYAGE TO THE PACIFIC OCEAN. Second edition, in three
          volumes. London: H. Hughs.

Curtis, Edward S.
1930   THE NORTH AMERICAN INDIAN. Volume 20. Nunivak, King Island,
       Little Diomede Island, Cape Prince of Wales, Kotzebue. Norwood:
       The Plimpton Press.

Davydov, G. I.
1977   TWO VOYAGES TO RUSSIAN AMERICA, 1802–1807. Translated by
       Colin Bearne, edited by Richard A. Pierce. Kingston: The Limestone
       Press.

Elliott, Henry W.
1886   OUR ARCTIC PROVINCE: Alaska and the Seal Islands. New York:
       Charles Scribner's Sons.

Gubser, Nicholas J.
1965   THE NUNAMIUT ESKIMOS: Hunters of Caribou. New Haven: Yale
       University Press.

Heath, John D.
1972   THE KING ISLAND KAYAK. Unpublished manuscript No. 1084.2 (35
       typescript pages of text, 54 pages of photos with captions). Archives
       of the Candian Ethnology Service, National Museum of Man, Ottawa.

Hooper, C. L.
1881   REPORT OF THE CRUISE OF THE U.S. REVENUE-STEAMER
       CORWIN. Washington: Government Printing Office.

Hrdlička, Aleš
1945   THE ALEUTIAN AND COMMANDER ISLANDS AND THEIR
       INHABITANTS. Philadelphia: The Wistar Institute of Anatomy and
       Biology.

Jochelson, Waldemar
1908   THE KORYAK. The Jesup North Pacific Expedition, Volume 6. Memoir
       10, American Museum of Natural History. Leiden: E.J. Brill.

1933   HISTORY, ETHNOLOGY AND ANTHROPOLOGY OF THE ALEUT.
       Washington: Carnegie Institution of Washington, Publication No.
       432.

de Laguna, Frederica
1956   CHUGACH PREHISTORY: The Archaeology of Prince William Sound,
       Alaska. Seattle: University of Washington Press.

von Langsdorff, G. H.
    1814   VOYAGES AND TRAVELS IN VARIOUS PARTS OF THE WORLD
              DURING THE YEARS 1803, 1804, 1805, 1806 AND 1807. In two
              volumes. London: Henry Colburn.

Lantis, Margaret
   1933–34 ATKA FIELD NOTES, 1933–34. Unpublished field notes on kayaks
              and kayak travel (23 typescript pages). Zimmerly kayak files.

    1946   THE SOCIAL CULTURE OF THE NUNIVAK ESKIMO. Transactions of
              the American Philosophical Society 35(3): 153–323.

Lisiansky, Urey
    1814   A VOYAGE ROUND THE WORLD IN THE YEARS 1803, 4, 5 & 6.
              London: John Booth.

Mathers, Charles W.
    1972   A TRIP TO THE ARCTIC CIRCLE. Originally published in *Farmers
              Advocate*, Winnipeg, Dec. 21, 1903. *Alberta Historical Review*
              20(4):6–15.

McGhee, Robert
    1972   BELUGA HUNTERS: An Archaeological Reconstruction of the History
              and Culture of the Mackenzie Delta Kittegaryumiut. Newfoundland
              Social and Economic Studies No. 13. Toronto: University of Toronto
              Press.

Menovshchikov, G.A.
    1959   ESKIMOSY. (A popular-scientific historico-ethnographic sketch on the
              Asiatic Eskimos). (Original: Eskimosy. Magadan: Magadanskoe
              Knizhnoe Izdatyelstvo). Unpublished English translation (five
              typescript pages), Library, National Museums of Canada, Ottawa.

Murdoch, John
    1892   ETHNOLOGICAL RESULTS OF THE POINT BARROW EXPEDITION.
              Ninth Annual Report of the Bureau of Ethnology, 1887–1888.
              Washington: Government Printing Office.

Nelson, Edward W.
    1899   THE ESKIMO ABOUT BERING STRAIT. Eighteenth Annnual Report of
              the Bureau of American Ethnology, 1896–1897. Washington:
              Government Printing Office.

Nelson, Richard K.

1966   ALASKAN ESKIMO EXPLOITATION OF THE SUMMER SEA ICE
        ENVIRONMENT. Unpublished 1966 study for Arctic Aeromedical
        Laboratory, Fort Wainwright, Alaska. Mimeo.

1969   HUNTERS OF THE NORTHERN ICE. Chicago: University of Chicago
        Press.

Nordenskiold, A. E.

1881   THE VOYAGE OF THE VEGA ROUND ASIA AND EUROPE. Two
        volumes. London: Macmillan and Co.

Nuligak

1966   I, NULIGAK. Maurice Metayer, trans. Toronto: Peter Martin
        Associates.

Petroff, Ivan

1884   REPORT ON THE POPULATION, INDUSTRIES AND RESOURCES
        OF ALASKA. In Tenth Census of the U.S. Washington: Government
        Printing Office.

Ray, Dorothy Jean

1966   THE ESKIMO OF ST. MICHAEL AND VICINITY AS RELATED BY
        H.M.W. EDMONDS. Anthropological Papers of the University of
        Alaska 13(2):1–143.

Rasmussen, Knud

1999   ACROSS ARCTIC AMERICA. NARRATIVE OF THE FIFTH THULE
        EXPEDITION. Fairbanks: University of Alaska Press.

Robert-Lamblin, Joelle

1980   THE ALEUT KAYAK—AS SEEN BY ITS BUILDER AND USER—AND
        THE SEA OTTER HUNT. (Original: Le kayak aléoute vu par son
        constructeur et utilisateur et la chasse à la loutre de mer. Tome 20,
        Fascicule 1, Objets et Mondes. Dieppe: Musée de l'homme, Mus.
        Nat. d'Histoire Naturelle). Unpublished English translation (20
        typescript pages), Library, National Museum of Canada, Ottawa.

Sauer, Martin

1802   AN ACCOUNT OF A GEOGRAPHICAL AND ASTRONOMICAL
        EXPEDITION TO THE NORTHERN PARTS OF RUSSIA. Performed by
        Commodore Joseph Billings, in the Years 1785, &c. to 1794. London:
        T. Cadell, Jun. and W. Davies, in the Strand.

Vdovin, I. S.

1973   STUDIES IN THE ETHNIC HISTORY OF THE KORYAKS. (Original:
        Ocherki Etnicheskoi Istorii Koryakov. Akademiya Nauk USSR, Institut
        Etnografi. Leningrad: Nauka Press). Unpublished English translation
        (13 typescript pages), Library, National Museums of Canada, Ottawa.

Veniaminov, Ivan Evsieevich Popov

1840   NOTES ON THE ISLANDS OF THE UNALASKA DISTRICT. (Original:
        Innokentii, Metropolitan of Moscow. Zapiaki ob ostrovakh
        Unalashkinskago otdela). St. Petersburg: Russian-American Company.
        Pp. 409; tables. Yale: Western Americana, Zc86. 840 in.v.2–3.

Zimmerly, David W.

1978   KAYAKS OF HOOPER BAY, ALASKA. In Contextual Studies of
        Material Culture. David W. Zimmerly, ed., pp. 27–44. Paper No. 43,
        Canadian Ethnology Service, Mercury Series. Ottawa: National
        Museum of Man.

1979   HOOPER BAY KAYAK CONSTRUCTION. Paper No. 53, Canadian
        Ethnology Service, Mercury Series. Ottawa: National Museum of
        Man. 118 pages.

1984   ARCTIC PADDLE DESIGN. *Sea Kayaker* 1(3):8–15.

1985   THE MACKENZIE ESKIMO KAYAK. *Sea Kayaker* 2(3):6–11.

INDEX

[page numbers of figures appear in brackets]

A

Adney, Edwin Tappan, 10, 74
Aigner, Jean S., 15
Akun Island, [16]. See also Aleutian Islands
Alaska Historical Library, [6, 23, 24, 25, 30]
Alaska Peninsula, 15
Alaska State Museum, [15, 18, 19, 20 26, 27, 28, 33, 42, 44, 47, 51, 57, 58, 63, 66, 75]
Aleut, 15–28, [15–28]
　ballast, 7, 25–26
　confusion with Pacific Eskimo, 29
　damage control, 27
　fishing, [24–25]
　hat, 19, [6, 16, 19]
　hunting, 22–24, [19, 20, 22, 23–24]
　kayak, comparison with Pacific Eskimo, 30, 35
　kayak, cultural context, 27–28
　kayak design, 7, 17–19, 20–23, 26, [15, 16, 17, 21, 22, 23]
　navigation, 26
　paddles, 25, 77, 79, [79]
　paddling techniques, 25
　speed secrets, 22–23, [22–23]
　warfare, 25
Aleutian Islands, 3, 6, 7, 15–28, 51, 74
　discovery and exploration, 15
American Museum of Natural History, [19, 78]
Amlia, 26
Anadyr River, 12–13. See also Chukchi
Anaktuvuk Pass, 69, 70
Anatkuat, 12, [12]. See also One-hole kayak
Anchorage Museum of History and Art, [30, 36, 38, 49, 62]
Anderson, R. M., [68]
Anguun, 57. See also Paddles, single-bladed
Anthropometric measurements, 37, 40, 44
Antropova, V. V., 11, 13
Archaeological dating, 3
Armstrong, Alexander, 73, 76
Arrows
　burial, 34
　storage, 36
　warfare, 25, 41
Atka, 26
Atlatl, [50]. See Throwing board
Avataq, 57. See also Float bag

B

Baffin Islands, 6
Baidarka, 15–38. See also Aleut; Eskimo, Pacific; Kayak
Bailer, 20, 27, 37, [27]
Baja California, 17
Baleen, 17, 30, 32, 75, 76. See also Whale
Ballast
　Aleut, 25–26
　game, 6
　Koryak, 10
　rock, 7, 10, 25–26, 57
Barter Island, 67, [68]
Baydar, 11. See also Umiak
Beam, 5, 6, 18, 20, 21–22, 29, 30, 41, 44–46, 55, 64, 68, 74, 79–80
Belkofsky Island, [20]
Beluga whale, 65–66, 71–73
Bering Sea, 39–52, [38–52]
　accessories, 42
　construction, 44–46
　Hooper Bay kayak, 43–46, [39, 43, 44–46]
　kayak design, 6, 41, 47–49, 51, [39, 48, 51]
　kayak uses, 43, 46, 49–51
　Norton Sound kayak, 47–49, [47–51]
　Nunivak Island kayak, 40–41, [39–42]
　paddles, 41, 50–51, 76, 79–80
　paddling techniques, 41, 50–51
Bering Strait, 53–62, [53–62]
　accessories, 57
　Cape Espenberg kayak, 55, [56]
　capsize recovery, 59, [59–60]
　freighting, 61–62
　hunting, 58, 60–61
　kayak design, 6, 54–55, 62, [53–55, 62]
　King Island kayak, 56, [53–56, 57]
　paddles, 76, 81, [79]
Bering, Vitus, 15
Bilge, 41
　stringers, 74
Birds
　eagle feathers, 75
　eggs, 11
　hunting, 4, 35, 40, 42, 43, 49
Birket-Smith, Kaj, 35–37
Black, Lydia T., 33–35
Bladder. See also Float bag
　Aleuts, 7, 27
　Bering Sea, 42
　Kodiak Eskimo, 34

Bogoras, Waldemar, 9, 12, 14
Bone
  deck loops, 76, [74]
  joints, 22–23, [22–23]
  on paddles, [78]
  sled runners, [57]
Bow, kayak, 17–18, 55, 68, 71, 74, [15, 16, 31, 38, 41,
      47, 71]
  bifid, 18, [15, 16, 29, 31–32]
Brevig Mission, 54
Brooks Range, 69
Bunyan, Dick, 44–46, 79, [39, 45–46, 73]
Burg, Amos, [53]
Burial, 28, 34

C

Cadiak. See Eskimo, Kodiak
Camden Bay, [68]
Canadian Museum of Civilization, 74, [9, 12, 13, 16, 17,
      21, 29, 31–32, 39, 48, 64, 67, 70, 75]
Canoe, displacing kayak in use, 14
Canteen, 7, 42
Cape Espenberg, 54–55, [55]
Capsize recovery techniques, [83–90]. See also Survival
      techniques
  Aleut, 25, 27, 28
  alternatives, 27, 59
  Bering Strait, 59
  Chugach, 37
  Greenland, 6
  King Island, 59
  Kotzebue, 66
  lack of, 6
  Nunivak, 42
  single-bladed, 6, 59
  team rescue, 7
  two-hole and three-hole, 37
Caribou
  hunting, 4, 5, 64, 66, 67, 69, 71
  skins, kayak construction, 64, 70, 77
Carrying capacity, kayak, 6, 43, 49
Carrying handles, 10, 47, 51, 55, [51]
Catamaran technique
  freighting, 60–62
  sail, 42, 50
  survival, 7, 30, 34
  trading, 61–62, [61]
Cedar. See Wood
Ceremony. See Ritual

Chapelle, Howard I., 10, 74
Chenega, 35
China, 15
Chine, 5, 6, 7, 54, 63, 74
Choris, Louis, [6, 15, 19]
Christianity, 46
Chukchi, 3, 4, 7, 9, 12–14
  inland kayak, 3, 12–14, [13]
  maritime kayak, 12–13, [12]
  paddles, 72
Chukchi Peninsula, 13
Chukotka Peninsula, 12
Clothing. See Hat; Mitts; Parka
Coaming, 6, 12, 20, 37, 42, 44–46, 48, 55, 63, 74, [46]
Cockpit, 4, 6, 7, 10, 14, 22, 31, 41, 43, 49, 54, 61–62, 63,
      64, 68, 70, 74, 75, 76, 77, [43]
Colnett, Captain J., 35
Communication
  hunting, 33, [23]
  traveling, 26
Conservation of kayaks, 4, 49
Construction, kayak, 20, 22–23, 29–30, 35–36, 40–41,
      44–46, 54–55, 63–64, 70, 74–75, 76, [44–46]
  materials, 35–36. See also Skins; Wood
    baleen, 17, 30, 32, 42, 75, 76
    bone, 22–23,[22–23, 75]
    oils, 20, 36
    paint, 20, 45, 46
    sinew, 3, 20, 46, 75
    tallow, 70
  ritual, 40–41
  time, 20, 46
  tools, 36, 44, 45
  twentieth century, 35, 70
Cook, James, 16, 17, 18, 35
Cross section. See Design, cross section
Curtis, Edward S., 40–41, 53, 60, 65–66, [41, 63]

D

Dame, Ray B., [49]
Danish National Museum, 74, [29, 58, 60]
Dart, 22–23, [22, 51]. See also Harpoon; Javelin; Spear
  bird, 3, 35, 57
  sea otter, 33
  whale, 34
Daughhetee, Mark, [15, 18, 21, 27, 33, 42, 47, 51, 54, 57,
      65, 66, 81]
Davydov, G. I., 34, 37
Death
  burial, 28, 34

Death(continued)
  epidemics, 74
  hunting, 34
Deck
  beams, 18, 30, 44–45, 55, 68, 74, [22]
  construction, 40–41, 44–45, 74
Deck loops, 76, [75]
Decoration
  clothing, [19, 26, 52]
  gear, 75, [57]
  kayak, 18, 20, [40, 41]
  paddles, 75–76, 79–82, [80, 81]
Deer. See Caribou; Reindeer
DeRoux, Ken, [52]
Design, kayak. See also regional entries; One-hole kayak;
    Three-hole kayak; Two-hole kayak
  cross section
    concave, 18
    flat, 6, 41
    round, 5, 63, 71, 74, 75,
    V-shaped, 6, 7, 10, 14
  drawings, [9, 12, 13, 16, 17, 21, 29, 31–32, 39, 48, 53,
    64, 67, 70, 71]
  sheer, 45–46, 48, 64, 70, 74
  speed, 5, 7, 14, 22–23, 25, 41, 63, 65, 66, 77
  stability, 6, 48, 67, 79–80
    ballast, 7, 10, 25, 57
    poor, 6, 7, 10–11, 14, 25, 63
Deterioration of kayaks, 4, 32
Diomede Islands, 14, 61. See also Eskimo, Siberian
Dutch Harbor. See Unalaska

E

East Cape, Siberia, 3, 14
Edmonds, H.M.W., 47–51
Education
  harpoon use, 27–28
  hunting, 27–28, 35
  kayak construction, 40
Elliot, Henry W., 56, [23–25]
Eskimo, Asiatic. See Eskimo, Siberian
Eskimo, Caribou, 5
Eskimo, Chugach, 35–37
  accessories, 36
  confusion with Aleuts, 29
  kayak construction, 35–36, 37
  kayak design, 30, 35, [35]
  kayak use, 35, 36
  paddles, 37, 79

  paddling technique, 37
Eskimo, Copper
  kayak, 71
  paddle, 68
Eskimo, Kodiak, 30–35
  education, 35
  hunting
    sea otter, 33
    whale, 33–34
    Russian management, 33–34
  kayak design, 30–32, [29, 31, 32]
  paddles, 34, 77, 79, [80]
  paddling technique, 34
  warfare, 25
Eskimo, Koniag. See Eskimo, Kodiak
Eskimo, Mackenzie, 71–76, 77
  history, 73–74
  hunting, 71–73
  kayak design, 74–75, [71, 74, 75]
  paddles, 75–76, 77
Eskimo, Nunamiut, 69–70
Eskimo, Pacific, 29–38. See also Eskimo, Kodiak; Eskimo,
    Chugach
  kayak design, 29–30, 56, [39, 40, 43, 45, 47, 48]
  paddles, 64–65, 79, [80]
Eskimo, Siberian
  kayaks, absence of, 14
  kayak design, 9
  language, 14
Ethnographic Museum of Sweden, [12]
European exploration, 35, 71. See also Missionaries;
    Russians; Traders, Whalers

F

Fishing, 4, 13, 35, 36, 43, 49, 53, 71, [24, 25, 38, 49]
Flint harpoon, 33, 66
Float bag. See also Bladder
  canteen, 7, 42
  harpoon line, use on, 50, 60–61, 75, [50]
  seal skin, 57
Float board. See Harpoon line and tray
Fort McPherson, [72]
Frame, kayak, 20, 35–36, 46, 75, [41, 42, 55]
Furs, 61, 62. See also Skins

G

Gaffs
  Bering Strait, 6
  storage, 42

Gear storage on kayak, 36, 42, 50, 57, 60, 62, 76, [20, 39, 51]
Gideon, Father, 33–34
Glenbow Museum, [54, 59–60, 61]
Greenland, 4, 5, 6, 14
Gubser, Nicholas J., 69
Gunnel. *See* Gunwale
Gunwale, 29, 36, 42, 45–46, 55, 61–62, 68, 69

H

Hale, Aloysius, [46]
Harpoon, [19, 50]. *See also* Dart; Hunting gear; Javelin; Spear; Throwing board
  construction, 20
  education in use, 27–28
  float bag, use with, 50, 60–61, 75, [50]
  harpoon line and tray, 50, 57, [57]
  hunting technique, 11, 23–24, 33, 60–61
  storage onboard, 36, 42, 57, 75, 76
Hat
  Aleut, 19, [6, 16, 19]
  Norton Sound, 50, [50, 52]
  value, 50
Heath, John D., 57, 59–62, 69, 81
Hemlock, 35–36
Holmberg, Heinrich J., [29]
Hooper Bay, 43–46, [39, 43–46]. *See also* Bering Sea
Hooper, C. L., 58, 61, 65, 66
Hrdlička, Aleš, 20, 25
Hudson Bay, 5
Hull, 32, 41, 63, 75. *See also* Design, kayak, cross section
Hunting
  birds, 4, 11, 35, 40, 42, 43, 49
  caribou, 4, 5, 64, 66–67, 69, 71
  commercial, 33–34. *See also* Traders
  education, 27, 28, 35
  gear, 36, 50, 57, 75–76
  marine mammals, 5, 11, 41, 57, 60–61, [6, 22, 23–24, 43]
  muskrat, 64
  ownership of kill, 24, 33, 72
  porpoise, 36
  reindeer, 13, 78, [5]
  seal, 4, 11, 13, 58, 60–61, 65, 67, 71, 78, 81, [6, 19, 43, 47, 65]
  sea otter, 15–17, 18, 22–24, 33, 79, [19, 20, 23]
  walrus, 4, 14, 58, 60–61
  whale, 4, 14, 33–34, 65–66, 71–73, 75, [19, 24, 31]

I

Ice, influence of, 5
Icy Cape, [66]
Indian, Southeast Alaska, 51
Inland kayak, 3, 4, 5, 13–14, 63–66, 69–70
Itkantsy, 11. *See also* Koryak
Ivory, 3, 23, 56, [42, 52, 57]

J

Jacket. *See* Parka
Javelin, 24. *See also* Dart; Harpoon; Spear
Jenness, Diamond, 74
Jochelson, Waldemar, 9, 10, 11, 15, 23, 25–26, [10]
Joints
  ball, 22–23, [22–23]
  keelson, 20, 23, 45–46, [23]
  mortise, 45, 68
  scarf, 23, 45–46, [23]

K

Kadiak, 25. *See also* Eskimo, Kodiak
Kamchatka Peninsula, 9, 11, 15
Kamentsy, 11. *See also* Koryak
Kamshadal, 9. *See also* Koryak
Karaginskiy Island, 11
Kayak
  artifacts surviving, 4, 9, 14, 30, 70, 74, 80
  carrying capacity, 6, 49
  comparison with other kayaks, 5, 25, 29, 30, 47, 51, 62, 64, 68, 71, [5]
  comparison with other watercraft, 10, 14, 29, 30, 70
  cooking utensils in, 20
  discontinuance of use, 14, 17, 46, 67, 69
  launching, 58, [58]
  maneuverability, 5, 10
  seaworthiness, 6, 18, 41, 83
  twentieth century, 4, 35, 43, 46, 69
  uses, 4. *See also* Fishing; Hunting; Transportation; Warfare
Keewatin, 5
Keelson, 20, 23, 45–46, 63, 68, 74–75, [16, 23]
King Island. *See also* Bering Strait
  barter goods, 56
  capsize recovery, 59–60
  kayak design, 51, 53–55, 56, 71 [53, 55]
  launching technique, 58
  origin, legend, 53
  Ookivok people, 56

King Island *(continued)*
  trading, 61
Kinship, Aleut, 27–28
Kitigariut, 72
Kneeplates, 37
Knicklick, 35, [35]
Kodiak Island, 29–35. *See also* Eskimo, Kodiak
Koryak, 4, 9–11, [9, 10]
  Karagintsy, 11
  kayak design, 7, 10, [9]
  hunting techniques, 11
  paddles, 11, 14, 78–79, [78]
Kotzebue Sound, 58, [64, 65]. *See also* North Alaska
  hunting techniques, 65–66
  kayak design, 64–65, [64, 65]
  trade fair, 61

L

Laguna, Frederica de, 35
Langsdorff, G. H. von, 11, 22
Language
  Eskimo and Aleut split, 3
  Siberian and Alaskan Eskimo, 14
  Yupik and Inupiat, 54
Lantis, Margaret, 20, 23, 26, 40, 41, [17]
Lanyard, use with paddles, 11, 78, [78]
Larsen, Helge, 3
Lashings, 3, 20, 32, 40, 46, 68, 75
LaVoy, Merle, 35
Legend
  King Island, origin of, 53
Lisiansky, Urey, 30, 32, 33, 34, [31–32]
Lomen Brothers, [54, 56, 59–60, 61]
Lowie Museum of Anthropology, [17, 48, 64]
Lubisher, Joseph, [22–23]
Luck, 40
  amulet, 65
  female, [40]
  objects in kayak, 41, 65, [18, 40]
  male, [40]
  representation, [40–41]
Lyon, G. F., [5]

M

Mackenzie River Delta, 5, 71, 74
Maleness
  kayak as living male, 28
  luck, good, [40]
  ownership of kayak, 35
Maneuverability, 5, 10
Marine mammals. *See* Hunting, marine mammals; Sea
    otter; Seal; Walrus; Whale
Maritime kayak, 5–7, 10–13, 15
Mat, grass, 42, [43]
McGhee, Robert, 71
Measurements
  construction, traditional, 37, 40–41
  construction, 20th century, 44–46
  documentation, 69, [7]
Menovshchikov, G. A., 3, 14
Missionaries, [28]
  Native culture, destruction of, 46
  three-hole kayak, demand, 22, 31, 35
Mitts, 42
Models, kayak, 3–4, 14, 51, [3, 18, 20, 27, 28, 33, 42, 47,
    51, 66]
Moses, Kivetyoruk, [58]
Murdoch, John, 66
Museum of Anthropology and Ethnology, [10, 16, 18, 31,
    80]
Museum of Ethnology of the Peoples of the USSR, [9, 13]
Museum, kayaks in. *See* Conservation; Deterioration;
    Storage
Muskrat hunting, 64

N

Nashoalook, 68
National Museums of Canada, 44, [39, 41, 44–47, 65, 71]
Navigation, 26
Nelson, Edward W., 47, 49, 50, 56, 62, [50]
Nelson Island, 45
Nelson, Richard K., 67, 68
Nikolski, [28]
Noatak River, 64
Nome, 54, 55, 74, [58]
Nordenskiold, A. E., 12, 78, [12, 80]
North Alaska, 63–70, [63–70]
  kayak design, 5, 63–64
  Kotzebue Sound/Point Barrow kayak
    kayak design, 64, [64–65]
    kayak use, 65
    hunting, whale, 65–66
    paddles, 82, [66, 81]
    paddling techniques, 66
  North Alaska retrieval kayak, 67–68, [67, 68]
  Nunamiut kayak
    hunting, caribou, 69

North Alaska (continued)
  Nunamiut kayak (continued)
    kayak design, 69, [69, 70]
    paddles, 66, 68, 82, [82]
Norton Sound kayak, 47–51, 64–69, [48]. See also St.
    Michael
Nuligak, 72–73, 75
Nunivak Island, 40, 44, [40, 41]. See also Hooper Bay

O

Oils, 36, 61
  seal, 20, 49
  shark liver, 36
Ookivok. See King Island
Oonalashka, [26]. See Unalaska
One-hole kayak, 15–18, 25–26, 33, 35, 36, 41, 49, 50,
    54, [5, 6, 9, 10, 12, 13, 14, 15, 16, 17, 29, 30, 38,
    39, 41, 42, 43, 48, 49, 50, 51, 53, 54, 55, 56, 58, 59–
    60, 61, 63, 64, 65, 66, 67, 68, 70, 71, 72, 73, 83]
  design development, 15
  use, 33, 34, 35, 36, 49
Ownership, hunting, 24, 33, 72

P

Paddle
  construction materials, 20, 77
  decoration, 75–76, 79–82
  double-bladed, 4, 11, 14, 25, 34, 37, 41, 51, 57, 66, 75–
    76, 77–82, [66, 78, 79, 81, 82, 83]
  drip rings, 75, 77
  length, 57, 77, 80, 81
  signaling with, 33, [23]
  single-bladed, 6, 11, 25, 34, 37, 41, 50–51, 57–59, 66,
    77–81, [80, 81]
  specialized
    hand, 11, 78–79, [10, 78, 79]
    lanyard tied, 11, 78, [10, 78]
    sculling, 41
    spear, 14, 78, [78]
  use in hunting, 33, 66, 72, [23]
Paddling
  sculling, 41, 78–79
  stability, 23, [22, 25]
  stealth, 5, 11
  technique, 11, 25, 34, 37, 41, 50–51, 59, 78–79
Paints
  kayak frame, 20, 45, 68
  paddles, 79–82

Paneak, Simon, 70, [69, 70]
Parentsy, 11
Parka, 11, 37, 41–42, 57, [19, 20, 59]
  capsize recovery, role in, 37, 59
  Greenland, 6
  ritual, protective powers, 41
Parry, W.E., [5]
Pautik, 57. See also Paddle, double-bladed
Peabody Museum, [73]
Petroff, Ivan, 23
Point Barrow, 65, 66, 70, 71. See also Kotzebue Sound;
    North Alaska
Point Hope, 68
Prince William Sound, 29, 35, [35]
Public Archives of Canada, [66, 72]

R

Raincoat, gutskin. See Parka
Rasmussen, Knud, 74
Ray, Dorothy Jean, 29, 47–51, 65, [55]
Reindeer
  construction materials, 13, 76
  hunting, 13, 14, 78, [5]
Repairs, 27, 76
Ribs, kayak, 20, 29, 32, 45–46, 55, 63, 64, 68
Rifle, 60, 61, 67, 78–80, [20, 22, 43, 47]
Ritual
  burial, 28, 34
  hunting beluga whale, 65–66
  kayak construction, 40–41
Robert-Lamblin, Joelle, 17, 18, 19, 20, 27–28
Rocker, 5, 14, 46, 63
Rocks. See Ballast
Rolls. See Capsize recovery
Rudder, 26
Russian influences. See also Missionaries; Traders
  confusion between Aleut and Pacific Eskimos, 29
  sea otter trade, 15–17
  three-hole kayak, 17, 22, 30, 31, 35
  whale hunting, 33–34

S

Sail, 11
  Aleut, 26
  catamaran technique, 42, 50
  Koryak, 11
  Norton Sound, 50
  Nunivak/Hooper Bay, 42

St. Lawrence Island, 14, 56
St. Michael, 47–49, 50
St. Michael kayak, 51
Sarycev, 20, 25
Sauer, Martin, 18, 19
Sea kayak. *See* Maritime kayak
Sea lion, construction materials, 20, 27, 36
Sea otter
  hunting
    methods, 15–17, 22, 23–24, 33, [23]
    prohibition, 17
    Russian organization, 15–17, 33
    skins, 15
    spirit of being, 23, [18]
Seal, 67, 78. *See also* Hunting, seal; Skins, seal
  bearded, 42, 55, 57, 58
  hair, 40
  oil, 20, 49
  spotted, 36, 40, [43]
  stomach, 27, 42
Seward Peninsula, 3, 54
Sheldon Jackson Museum, [15, 42, 52, 54, 56, 65]
Shishmaref, 54
Siberia, 3–4, 9–14
Sill, Jesse, [53]
Sinew, 3, 20, 46, 75
Skins. *See also* Furs
  caribou, 64, 70
  reindeer, 13, 61
  seal, 20, 36, 42, 55, 74
  sea lion, 20, 36
  sea otter, 15
  walrus, 55, 61
Skin sewing, 20, 40, 70, 76
Slaves, 19
Sled, 42, 57, 60, 65, 67, [42, 43, 55, 57, 61, 65, 66]
Smithsonian Institution
  National Anthropological Archives, [35, 39, 50, 51]
  National Museum, [21, 79]
Sokolnikov, N. I., 13
Songs, 40, 41
Sovoroff, Sergie, [37]
Spear. *See also* Dart; Harpoon; Javelin; Paddle, specialized
  beluga whale hunting, 33, 66
  bird, 76
  caribou hunting, 69
  substitute paddle, 51
Spear thrower, 20. *See also* Throwing board
Speed. *See* Design, speed
Speed secrets, 22–23, [22–23]

Spirit
  kayak, 18, 28
  sea otter, 23
Spray skirt, 30, 57, 63, [22]
Spruce. *See* Wood
Stability. *See* Design, stability; Paddling, stability
Stanchion, 46, 61. *See also* Gunwale
  decoration, [18, 40]
Stealth. *See* Paddling, stealth
Stern, 5, 25, 29, 35, 37, 55, 68, 70, 74
Storage, 4, 49, [38, 49]
Storage of gear on kayak, 36, 42, 50, 57, 60, 62, 76 [20, 39, 51]
Stringers, 42. *See also* Gunwale; Keelson
  bilge, 74
  deck, 10, 45, 55, 74
  longitudinal, 10, 63–64, 68, 74
Survival techniques. *See also* Capsize recovery
  after capsizing, 59
  catamaran, 7, 30, 34
  team rescue, 7
Symbolism. *See also* Decoration; Tradition
  kayak design, 18, [18, 40, 41]

T

Taboo, 46
Tattoo, 73
Thomas Burke Memorial Washington State Museum, 22, [22–23]
Three-hole kayak, 15–17, 21, 22, 23, 30, 31–32, 35, 36, 37, 51, [21, 22, 28, 30, 33, 34, 35, 36, 47]
  design development, 22, 31, 35, 51
  use, 22, 31, 35
Throwing board, 3, 20, 50, 57, [19, 50, 57]
Toggle systems, 6
Tomaganak, Silas, [43]
Tools, kayak construction, 36, 44, 45
Traders, influence. *See also* Russian influences
  casualties, 34
  hunting parties, 15–17, 33–34
  rifle, 60, 61, 67, 79–80
  sea otter, 15–17, 22
  three-hole kayak design, 17, 22, 30, 31, 35
  whale, 33–34
Trading, 56, 61, [61]
Tradition
  amulet, 65
  building of kayak, 40–41, 45
  burial, 28, 34

Tradition *(continued)*
  capsized hunters, beluga whale hunt, 66
  feasting, 65
  kayak as hunting partner, 28
  kayak owner's helping spirit, 18, [41]
  hunter's self-image, 35
  ownership of kill, 24, 33, 72
  sea otter's spirit, 23
  rock ballast, return to land, 25–26
  tattoo, 73
Translucency of kayak, 19, 20
Transportation
  freight, 21–22, 31, 49, 50, 56, 61, 62, [39]
  game, 6, 60–61
  people, 4, 13, 21–22, 31, 35, 36, 43, 49, 56
Two-hole kayak, 13, 15, 21–22, 26, 28, 30, 33, 35, 36, 51,
    62, [18, 21, 22, 23, 24, 25, 27, 30, 33, 62]
  design development, 51, 62
  uses, 15, 22–24, 33, 34, 36

U

Ukinet. *See* Koryak, Karagintsy
Umiak, 3, 11, 44, 61, 65
Unalaska, 17, 18–19, 22, [21, 22–23, 26, 27]
United States National Archives, [22]
United States National Museum, [21]
University of Alaska Archives, [56]
University of Alaska Museum, [70]
University of Washington Instructional Media Production
    Services, [20, 34]
University Museum, University of Pennsylvania, [40, 67,
    68]

V

Value
  hat, 19, 50
  kayak, 35, 40
Vdovin, I. S., 10, 11
Veniaminov, Ivan Evsieevich Popov, 18, 19, 21–22, 23–25,
    27
Voznesenskii, I. G., 11, [16]

W

Wales, 54
Wallen, R. T., [53]
Walrus
  hunting, 4, 14, 58, 60–61
  skins, 55, 61
Warfare, 25, 41
Waterproofing, 20, 36, 70, 76
Webber, John, [16]
Whale
  baleen, 17, 32, 75, 76
  beluga, 56, 65–66, 71–73
  humpback, [24]
  hunting, 4, 14, 33–34, 65–66, 71–73
Whalebone, 30. *See also* Baleen
Whalers, 61, 74
Women
  clamming, 43
  kayak construction, 40–41, 76
  luck, bad, 40–41, [40]
  wife, kayak needed for, 40
Wood, construction materials
  birch, 55
  cedar, 10, 20
  driftwood, 20, 44, 77
  hemlock, 35–36
  spruce, 35–36, 55, 75
    black, 20, 76, 77
    Canadian white, 70
    roots, 55, 75
  willow, 55, 70
Wound plugs, 61, [57]
Wute'en, 14

Y/Z

Yukon-Kuskokwim Delta, 40, 44
Zimmerly, David, 44, [27, 31, 43, 44–47, 68, 74]